RICHARD JEFFERIES

In an enchanting used bookstore in Stonington, Maine, Brooke and Terry Tempest Williams came across a rare copy of *The Story of My Heart*, an autobiography by nineteenth-century British nature writer Richard Jefferies. Considered a nature mystic by his contemporaries, Jefferies developed his understanding of "a soul-life" while wandering the wild countryside of Wiltshire, England. Brooke and Terry, like John Fowles, Henry Miller, and Rachel Carson before, were inspired by the prescient words of this little-known writer, who describes ineffable feelings of being at one with nature. In a foreword and responses set alongside Jefferies' writing, the Williams share their personal pilgrimage to Wiltshire to understand this man of "cosmic consciousness." Their exploration of Jefferies deepens their own relationship while illuminating dilemmas of modernity, the intrinsic need for wildness, and what it means to be human in the twenty-first century.

THE STORY
OF MY HEART

by Richard Jefferies
as rediscovered by
Brooke Williams and Terry Tempest Williams

≈

Afterword by Scott Slovic

TORREY HOUSE PRESS, LLC

SALT LAKE CITY • TORREY

First Torrey House Press Edition, November 2014
Copyright © 2014 by Brooke Williams and Terry Tempest Williams

Published by Torrey House Press, LLC
Salt Lake City, Utah
www.torreyhouse.com

International Standard Book Number: 978-1-937226-41-1
Library of Congress Control Number: 2014939595

Cover design by Rick Whipple, Sky Island Studio
Interior design by Jeff Fuller, Shelfish • Shelfish.weebly.com

Excerpts from essays published in *Ecopsychology*, June, 2014 (pp
122-123); and "The Colorado Archetypal River" published in *Desert
Water*, University of Utah Press, 2014, appeared in endnotes in slightly
different form.

Dedicated to Kathryn Blackett Tempest

How willingly I would strew the path of all with flowers;
how beautiful a delight to make the world joyous!
The song should never remain silent, the dance never still,
the laugh should sound like water which runs forever.

～

How pleasant it would be each day to think To-day
I have done something that will render future
generations more happy.

～

I will search the world for beauty.

RICHARD JEFFERIES
The Story of My Heart, 1883

CONTENTS

THE STORY
OF MY HEART

OBSESSION
Terry Tempest Williams

THE BOOK

The story of my heart is complicated. I suspect this is true for all of us. So when I found a small brown book with this title embossed in gold, I immediately picked it up and began reading the first page.

> My heart was dusty, parched for want of the rain of deep feeling; my mind arid and dry, for there is a dust which settles on the heart as well as that which falls on a ledge. It is injurious to the mind as well as to the body to be always in one place and always surrounded by the same circumstances. A species of thick clothing slowly grows about the mind, the pores are choked, little habits become a part of existence, and by degrees the mind is enclosed in a husk.

Who was this author and when was it published? I flipped back to the title page: Richard Jefferies, 1883. England. I had never heard of him. I continued reading:

> With all the intensity of feeling which exalted me, all the intense communion I held with the earth, the sun and sky, the stars hidden by the light, with the ocean—in no manner can the thrilling depth of these feelings be written— with these I prayed, as if they were the keys of an instrument...I swelled forth the notes of my soul, redoubling my own voice by their power...

Here was a writer akin to Whitman, to Emerson,

to Margaret Fuller and Thoreau. I recognized my own hunger in his desire to describe the ineffable. I also recognized how words fail us when trying to write about nature and in Jefferies' words, "the soul-life" that he was so desperate to convey.

My eyes have no fidelity on the page. They wander at will. If bored, they stop, but as I continued reading sentence after sentence, *Touching the crumble of earth, the blade of grass…thinking of the sea…* I was rapt, my eyes in sympathy with each florid page. Jefferies had my attention. Word after word, I kept following him while standing in a musty, used bookshop in Stonington, Maine.

Brooke was restless, ready to go, and found me in the corner with Richard Jefferies.

I showed him the book. Read him some passages. He listened and as he listened, calmed down.

"Who is this writer?" he asked. I shook my head. Brooke took the book in hand and opened the cover. "It's seventy-five bucks," he said. "We should find out more about him before we buy it."

And then, we left.

I kept thinking about that small, thin book. What would propel an Englishman in the nineteenth century to write such a personal account about his soul intertwined with nature and with such longing?

Had Richard Jefferies been influenced by the Transcendentalists? Or was he more closely aligned with the British romanticism of William Wordsworth and Samuel Coleridge? Or was he more philosopher or naturalist in the lineage of the great ornithologist Gilbert White? I felt like I had just located a lost relative through the genealogy of a genre, a genre that remains undefined and undervalued. Critics continue to be embarrassed by a passion for nature and a call for reflection, especially if it has to do with the body and the body politic.

Brooke and I were walking along a beach of Deer Isle, each of us content in our own thoughts. It was Labor Day weekend in Maine and unexpectedly, we had this particular beach to ourselves.

The next weekend was my birthday. We returned to the bookstore and there in the corner *The Story of My Heart* remained. This time, we noticed a handwritten sign, "All prices are negotiable." Brooke asked the elderly woman hidden behind piles of books on a wooden stool, pleasant enough, if this book, in particular, might be purchased for less than the penciled price marked inside.

"Did you get it over there?" she asked, pointing to the cabinet in the corner. Neither one of us had appreciated the elaborately carved bookcase made of black walnut.

"Everything in that cabinet is sixty-six percent off," she said.

Brooke pulled out his wallet and paid her $25.50.

"Happy birthday," he said.

THE READING OF THE BOOK

In a long marriage such as ours, Brooke and I often wonder about the balance between what we imagine to be true and what is actually *the truth*. The story that Brooke and I tell ourselves about first reading *The Story of My Heart* is this:

After we purchased the book, we read it to each other on the rocky shore of Goose Cove on Deer Isle. It's a favorite place of ours, a Nature Conservancy site enjoyed by many.

It was low tide, the sandy stretch of beach that links two islands was open. We found a flat ledge of pink granite and laid down together, my head on Brooke's chest, as he read the first three chapters from beginning to end until high tide reached us and we were forced to leave.

The swish of the surf, the small oscillations of the sea acted as punctuation marks to the cries of gulls carried by the breeze. Sometimes, while Brooke was reading, I would focus on the rolling horizon, watching sailboats pass or the occasional lobsterman pulling in traps from a sea of buoys that cover the blue waters like confetti. My mind would drift and then, a beautiful or evocative sentence would call me back because of its unexpected exuberance. Or a fly would create a disturbance. Or Brooke would stumble over an odd construction of Jefferies', slow down, and reread it.

Sometimes, we would stop mid-page to talk about a particular phrase and analyze it, either because we had felt that way, too, or we found it overwrought and overwritten, an homage to self-pity. And then, there were the moments when we sat upright and read the passage again, marveling over the power and poignancy of Richard Jefferies' perception.

This is how I remember the romance of that day when we first read *The Story of My Heart* out loud, outside, together.

Here is *the truth* of that day as recorded in my journal:

Today, Brooke and I spent a sublime day at Goose Cove, one of our favorite trails through the hushed forest. I took off my shoes and walked barefoot on the lush spongy moss, one of the great delights of my life literally bouncing on the floor of the forest deep and rich and vibrant green dotted with white luminous mushroom. To a desert dweller, this much green, this much water is a fantasy.

Once at the beach, we found a great perch on the pink granite rocks. So in awe of the clarity of the day, the iconic beauty of the islands, pink geometric blocks floating above the blue sea, where the middle landscape of islands populated by green spruce and firs—dense against cobalt sea and sky with wisps of clouds—point upward—my heaven.

Brooke pulled out The Story of My Heart *from his pack as we lay on the rocks, my head on his chest facing the horizon. He began reading Richard Jefferies out loud as the sea whispered in the background with gulls.*

Eloquent, florid, effusive prose. No, make that ecstatic prose. Jefferies speaks to both of our wild hearts. He speaks of "soul-thoughts," how the external wonder of the world ignites his inner world and you have the sense that while his outer body is very still, his inner life is on fire.

I loved the passage of him being tied to the molten core of the Earth, yet able to feel the reach of the stars. He desires his self to be this expansive, his intellect wide and in communion with the beauty that surrounds him. He wishes to write a "new book of the soul…a book drawn from the present and future, not the past. Instead of a set of ideas based on tradition, let me give the mind a new thought drawn straight from the wondrous present, direct this very hour."

We also loved what he had to say about idleness and leisure, the import of dreaming by the sea which was exactly what we were doing: Brooke sitting against the pink wall of granite; me, flat on my back, eyes closed, arms outstretched like a cross; sun beating down, no one around but the gulls and the loons and an albino guillemot playing in the surf at low tide, visible in the light only through a different kind of motion.

Rachel Carson is reported to have had two books by her bed stand at all times: *Walden* and *The Story of My Heart*. Henry Beston, author of *The Outermost House*, was also a fan of Richard Jefferies. Both of these "nature writers" lived in Maine. They were friends. I wonder how and when *The Story of My Heart* came into their lives, and with whom did they read these electric pages, and where?

THE MAN BEHIND THE BOOK

Our interest in Richard Jefferies grew. He was born in Swindon, England, in 1848.

His family farmed. He was a free spirit and ran away from home when he was fourteen years old. When he finally returned from his adventures at sea and in Paris, he spent the rest of his life roaming close to his farm in Coates.

Jefferies wrote. He wrote voraciously, prodigiously. Putting pen to paper for Jefferies was like breathing and every bit as necessary. We learned he had written more than five hundred essays, nineteen books (including nine novels), and five more books published posthumously. He died of tuberculosis in 1887. He was survived by his wife of thirteen years, Jessie Baden.

The British literary scholar H.S. Salt wrote shortly after his death, "There are few figures more pathetic or more heroic in the annals of our literature than that of this solitary, unfortunate brave-hearted man, who with 'three great giants' as he recorded in his journal, 'disease, despair, and poverty' could yet nourish to the last an indomitable confidence in the happiness of the future race." *The Guardian* recently called Jefferies, "arguably the founding father of British environmentalism," reporting on the irony of development threats near his family farm in Coate, England, where he would "ramble, wait, and watch."

In the winter of 2013, Brooke and I visited the Jefferies farm near the Coate Reservoir, bordered by woods animated by rooks and robins, blue-bridled tits, and squirrels, not far from the town of Swindon. The old farmhouse, now a museum, is only open once a week and less in the winter, but as luck would have it, the day we were there the six members of the Richard Jefferies Society were conducting their annual meeting and they welcomed us inside with tea and biscuits.

We wandered through the museum noting the various busts and portraits of Jefferies. His eyes in all mediums were intense and haunting. There were cases of artifacts from Ice Age spear points to hammer stones. Locks of hair, letters, a pocket watch were also on display. Natural history dioramas were plentiful from an era long gone. I was especially drawn to the snowy egrets with their gold painted feet. And up the staircase were the paintings of Kate Tryon, an artist from Naples, Maine, born in 1864, whose obsession with Richard Jefferies in the early 1900s was not unlike our own. She visited the Coate landscape with a desire to paint the places that had inspired Jefferies, pastoral settings where his poetic prose were written. A pleinair painter fell in love with a pleinair writer.

But the place of power in the museum where the spirit of Richard Jefferies spoke to us was on the third floor in the attic where the curators had reconstructed his childhood bedroom. It wasn't the mannequin of Richard as a boy (black-knickered, white-shirted, and suspendered) lying on his brass bed reading a book with his chin resting on his hand that moved us. Nor was it the rabid-looking red fox, badly mounted, with a snide grin perched on the wooden chest. What moved us was his writing desk, a simple drop-leaf piece of furniture made from pine with thin tapered legs situated in front of the window framed by blue curtains. A small chair with a wicker seat was tucked inside. The window was open. The curtains billowed. There was a vitality here I felt nowhere else.

"To be beautiful and to be calm without mental fear is the ideal of Nature," Richard Jefferies wrote. "If I cannot achieve it, at least I can think it."

Back home, we continued to reread *The Story of My Heart*. We became obsessed with bringing this book back into print so another generation could encounter his ideas. Ideas like the importance of being idle:

> I hope succeeding generations will be able to be idle. I hope that nine-tenths of their time will be leisure time; that they may enjoy their days, and the earth, and the beauty of this beautiful world; that they may rest by the sea and dream; that they may dance and sing, and eat and drink. I will work towards that end with all my heart. If employment they must have—and the restlessness of the mind will require it… They shall not work for bread, but for their souls.

Ideas like humility and the value of Earth's indifference:

> There is nothing human in nature. The earth, though loved so dearly, would let me perish on the ground, and neither bring forth food nor water.

Ideas relevant to the discussion of a sustainable life:

> I verily believe that the earth in one year produces enough food to last for thirty. Why then, have we not enough?

When Richard Jefferies says, "The circle of ideas we possess is too limited to aid us. We need ideas as far outside our circle as are outside those that were pondered by Augustus Caesar," I believe him.

But my growing kinship with Richard Jefferies as a fellow writer of natural history and memoir paled next to my husband's relationship with him. Day and night, Brooke was reading Jefferies. Night and day, he was quoting him. *A river runs itself clear in the night.* In other words, goodnight. And this: *Let me be fleshly perfect.* Translation: I need to go exercise. It got to the point that before leaving home, whether we were going to dinner with friends or to any public gathering, be it a party or a political hearing, Brooke had to promise me he would not bring up Richard Jefferies. Promise after promise was broken. No matter the occasion, Brooke managed to insert Jefferies into the conversation. I began to believe that Brooke and Jefferies were a ventriloquist team. I could no longer tell where Brooke's voice ended and Jefferies' voice began.

In the end, I gave up. I simply set a place for Jefferies at the table and let the two of them talk endlessly over breakfast, lunch, and dinner without Brooke ever moving his mouth. It was the look in his eyes. He was a thousand miles away.

But isn't that how marriages go, we survive one another's obsessions be it a person, place, or thing. Marriage is the accommodation of nouns. Brooke has survived my love affairs with Hieronymus Bosch, Philip II, and prairie dogs. He has traveled with me to Rwanda and returned home with a son. He has endured the re-enactment of the battle at Gettysburg and attended a Civil War ball. And early on in our marriage, he didn't say a word when I told him I would be gone for several months studying ophiuroids in the Gulf of California, nor did he balk at our growing library focused on death and dying.

Likewise, I have learned to live with his passions: backcountry skiing, wet wool, two dogs, and dragonflies. Because of Brooke's obsession with dragonflies, I now know how to distinguish meadowhawks from darners, darners from skimmers, and skimmers from sand dragons. And the absolute certainty that whenever we find ourselves in a landscape of stray rocks (often), Brooke will turn them into standing stones;

sculptures perfectly poised on the edge of a river or lake or ocean regardless of the occasion, including wakes and weddings.

I knew the how of Brooke's obsession with Jefferies; I had been part of it. What I didn't know was the why.

Last fall, we returned to Maine as we do each year. Richard Jefferies traveled with us. And once again, we read *The Story of My Heart* out loud outside. But something had changed. This time, when Brooke read the words of Richard Jefferies he was no longer reading them with a sense of curiosity and astonishment, he was reading them alive. He was reading them passionately, lyrically, and when called for, emphatically. *I burn life like a torch. The hot light shot back from the sea scorches my cheek—my life is burning in me. The soul throbs like the sea for a larger life. No thought which I have ever had has satisfied my soul.* He exhorted the ocean to answer Jefferies' questions: *Why then, do we not have enough?* When a gull landed near us on the granite slabs of Schoodic Point, Brooke faced the gull and read, *Let me be in myself myself fully.* Will you believe me when I say the Herring gull nodded? *With all the subtle power of the great sea, there rises an equal desire. Give me life strong and full as the brimming ocean; give me thoughts wide as its plane; give me a soul beyond these... The sea thinks for me as I listen and ponder; the sea thinks, and every boom of the wave repeats my prayer.*

Brooke was no longer reading the words of Richard Jefferies. He embodied them.

Give me bodily life equal in fullness to the strength of earth, and sun, and sea; give me the soul-life of my desire. Once more I went down to the sea, touched it and said, farewell. So deep was the inhalation of this life that day, that it seemed to remain in me for years. This was a real pilgrimage.

This was our pilgrimage.

This was the grist of our marriage—to explore, to experiment, to experience life.

This is why I remain in love with Brooke. My clear, meandering Brooke.

He was face to face with the earth, with the sun, the night; face to face with himself. There was nothing between. No wall of written tradition. No built-up system of culture—his naked mind was confronted with naked earth.

My Maine journal reads:

Brooke lies naked on rock. Sunlight squinting. Blue water. Ocher rockweed. Tide rising. Perfect day.

The world says no to this kind of living every day. We are told it is self-indulgent, naïve, a waste of time, and especially heartbreaking to me, "silly." We are told this kind of life belongs to the privileged. But Richard Jefferies was anything but privileged. He was a poor ecstatic eccentric who could barely put food on his table, yet he was full. Every day of his young life, he was full—full of wonder, full of questions, full of empathy and concern for the state of the world he believed was intrinsically tied to the state of his soul. He cared about the working man, the laborer, the yeoman, the woman making bread, and the child who would eat it. And he wrote voraciously about the virtues of country living. When Richard Jefferies wrote, *It is sweet on awaking in the early morn to listen to the small bird singing in the tree,* he acknowledged this spring rite belongs to everyone. This is what we have forgotten. Earth gives of itself freely and asks nothing of us in return—save the return of our bodies, dust to dust.

But we have become so insular, so busy, and obsessed with a capitalistic work ethic to fuel our mindless consumption, we forego the blessing of birdsong. In the process of becoming civilized, we have become inhuman.

We believe we are exceptional. Richard Jefferies tells us, *Genius is nature.*

THE BODY

The Story of My Heart is a spiritual autobiography written by a man who lived to be thirty-eight years old, plagued with illness. He was familiar with suffering. No doubt the "dark night of the soul" that Joseph Campbell addresses in *The Hero With A Thousand Faces* was familiar terrain for Richard Jefferies.

The wheat is beautiful, but the human life is labour.

Both Brooke and I met Jefferies after crossing

the thresholds of our own night sea journeys. Brooke lives with chronic heart disease. I have a yearly brain scan for a cavernous hemangioma. Neither ailment nor predicament has limited our lives, but it has highlighted how we wish to live, choosing to be present with the time at hand, rather than plummeting into fear about the time we may lose. No one is guaranteed a future. One approaches sixty with an awareness that time is finite as far as our bodies are concerned. Perhaps this acceptance of death is what fuels the urgency one feels when reading Richard Jefferies. It also may be what allows a reader to suffer through his struggles on the page.

"My strength is not enough to fulfill my desire," he writes.

> If I had the strength of the ocean, and of the earth, the burning vigour of the sun implanted in my limbs…never have I had enough of it. I wearied long before I was satisfied…the thirst was still there.

Richard Jefferies was a man who suffered physical limitations. He was not a man who suffered limitations of the spirit. He became a harsh critic with little patience for the dull of heart, the robotic, the listless mind who falls asleep through apathy.

> The complacency with which the mass of people go about their daily task, absolutely indifferent to all other considerations, is appall-

ing in its concentrated stolidity. They do not intend wrong—they intend rightly: in truth, they work against the entire human race...If the whole of the dead in a hillside cemetery were called up alive from their tombs, and walked forth down into the valley, it would not rouse the mass of people...

Richard Jefferies was a champion of rigorous inquiry, a lover of beauty, and an advocate for natural and social justice. He was an advocate for the poor, a friend of farmers' rights in the rise of Britain's urbanization. "Never, never rest contended," he said.

And through his writings, it becomes clear, he never did.

Jefferies' belief in physical exertion gave him the psychic energy necessary to live a more examined life. He pushed himself every day. Walking was at the crux of his healing. Every day, he walked the same worn path in the woods around his home and found something new, day by day, season by season. He delighted in the reliability of what he saw by covering the same territory year by year. "How nothing changes," yet "everything changes." Little escaped his attention. "A fullness of physical life causes a deeper desire of soul-life," he said.

I believe it to be a sacred duty, incumbent on every one, man and woman, to add to and encourage their physical life, by exercise and in every manner...Each one of us should do some little part for the physical good of the race—health, strength, vigour.

Being married to a man whose physical life is intrinsically tied to his spiritual life, I understand Jefferies' obsession with "the exaltation of the body, mind, and soul." I have watched Brooke and my own obsessions of the body change over time. I don't remember the exact day Brooke quit skiing "the steep and deep" of the Wasatch Mountains, but I do remember how the letting go of snow was met by the companionship of a dog named Rio. The physical exertion of winter was not so much replaced by a Basenji, more wild than domestic, but explored through their daily walks, call them saunterings, in the redrock desert that seduced them farther into the canyons.

My own physical relationship to the land has largely been following Brooke. He was so strong, so focused, so driven, that I often lagged behind—I was distracted by birds, by plants, by tracks. But an unexpected gift emerged. I had the illusion I was walking in the woods or the desert or the beach alone. My life has been a protected solitude.

THE BODY OF THE WHITE HORSE

If Richard Jefferies is known by some as "a nature mystic," he comes by it through proximity. Avebury's circles of standing stones is not far from his family farm. The healing waters of Bath are near. And the white chalk horses of Oxfordshire are marked on the

hills of the countryside of his home ground. The Uffington Horse, in particular, inspired him.

> This sculptured White Horse is of a gigantic
> size and is represented at full gallop. It may
> be seen fourteen or fifteen miles off, it being
> formed by cutting away the turf down to the
> white chalk... Immediately beneath the figure
> of the horse is a conical mound, or barrow,
> known as the Dragon's mound; from a tra-
> dition that here St. George slew the dragon,
> whose blood was of so poisonous a nature that
> nothing has since grown upon its summit,
> which is bare, exposing the chalk.

Brooke and I visited the Uffington Horse. We
had seen photographic images of the stylized animal
linked to the Bronze Age (1000 – 700 BC), but nothing could have prepared us for what we encountered.

The day was overcast and gray, threatening rain.
We kept walking upward across the dry grasses of the
steep, yet undulating slope of White Horse Hill, looking over our shoulders frequently at the dramatic valley
below. It is a rippled landscape, part of the Ridgeway
Escarpment. Legend has it that inside the furrows left
by the Ice Age is where the White Horse feeds at night.

We kept walking with the belief that at some point,
we would be able to see the White Horse in its entirety,
"at full gallop" across the hill, as Jefferies describes.

But this was our surprise: It cannot be seen all at
once, only as a white line stretching across the hill for

over one hundred meters like a river of light.

To see the White Horse of Uffington, you must walk it into being. You see the horse with your feet.

Brooke walked ahead, down the horse's back, all the way to its tail, until he dropped out of sight, to find the flanks and legs. I stood close to the White Horse's eye, never on it so not to obscure its vision. It was a solid chalked circle, white, framed by bold rectangular lines that defined its face. With fog now swirling around me, two lines like an inverted "V" emerged from the face like breath.

I found the White Horse's ears and walked them from tip to tip, descending and ascending through a white chalked "U." I whispered my questions to the White Horse trusting she could hear: *Whose hands etched you into being to celebrate you in white? Were you carved on a small stone first, imagined in a dream? Who believed in you? And where do you run now when the dreams have disappeared?* And then, I sauntered down her neck, across her back until I joined Brooke at the white-lined underbelly of the equine image and together we could see the gate of her long, elegant legs stretching across the tawny hillside in winter.

The deep trenches dug into the hillside, then filled with crushed native chalk, were cared for and regularly cleaned—by hand. Locals told us that until the nineteenth century, the White Chalk Horse of Uffington was scoured every seven years through a ritualistic fair held on the hillside so the horse could remain visible.

This vigilance to keep the White Horse alive continues. Without this kind of care, the Uffington Horse would be obscured.

I think about the care of a marriage, what surfaces in love to be shared and cherished; and what remains hidden, personal and private, from abuse or neglect or survival.

"Remain. Be content. Go round and round and round in one barren path," writes Richard Jefferies.

Patterns emerge through relationships—horse or human. The art of the Uffington Horse is the art of marriage: mind married to imagination; a vision married to a practice; the engagement and execution of belief made whole for the eyes to behold and the heart to ponder.

For the rest of the afternoon in brisk weather, Brooke and I walked the outline of the Uffington Horse. The White Horse made of chalk is the outline of a marriage: when you are inside it, you can't see the beauty of the overall design. It is only from an aerial perspective that you can see its alchemical power.

The White Horse gallops.

THE HEART

The story of my heart is the story of trusting it. Finding that small gold-embossed book in a dusty corner in a bookshop in Maine has become part of this story, the ongoing story of my marriage to Brooke Spencer Williams, son of Rosemary Brandley and Rex

Winder Williams, Jr., son of Rex Winder Williams, Sr. and Helen Spencer, daughter of John Daniel Spencer who was married to a woman called Clicky, who was the daughter of Brigham Young. Ours is a genealogy of a people in a place rooted by a spiritual calling.

"Go higher than a god, deeper than prayer, and open a new day," writes Richard Jefferies. We left the calling of our people and found our calling in place. The words of Richard Jefferies appeared as a cairn standing in the desert. We followed him along an unexpected path of rocky coastlines and white horses chalked into the English countryside and back home again to a renewed marriage of two minds embodied in wonder and that has made all the difference.

In discovering Richard Jefferies for ourselves, we discovered a fellow traveler of the wild, the beautiful, and the gentile. We found a soul mate in our search for a soul-life. In this new edition of *The Story of My Heart,* Brooke follows each of Jefferies' chapters with his own commentary, sometimes in agreement with the writer and sometimes not—consider it part of our ongoing conversation. We hope this book will matter to a new generation of Jeffries readers, if for no other reason than to rediscover what it feels like to fall back in love with the world.

Recently, I read Alan Lightman's opinion piece in *The New York Times,* "Our Lonely Home in Nature." He writes, "Nature is purposeless. Nature simply is. We may find nature beautiful or terrible, but those are human constructions. Such utter and complete mind-lessness is hard for us to accept. We feel such a strong connection in nature. But the relationship between nature and us is one-sided. There is no reciprocity... Nature can survive far more than what we can do to it and is totally oblivious to whether homo sapiens live or die in the next hundred years. Our concern should be about protecting ourselves—because we have only ourselves to protect."

What strikes me about Alan Lightman's declaration is its arrogance. Are we really the only species that deserves our care? By "protecting ourselves only," we don't have to feel, much less see, the unprecedented harm we are rendering to the planet. We proclaim our narcissistic nature void of empathy.

I choose to see Earth as a self-sustaining, self-correcting organism that responds to life, interconnected and interrelated. We are part of this mosaic of life. I do believe in the sentience of other species and I believe in the reciprocity of our relations beyond our own kind. I have experienced it repeatedly, whether it is a Galapagos fur seal blowing bubbles in front of me as we are swimming underwater and I blow bubbles back to him in a gesture of play—or when I call forth chickadees on a summer morning and find myself surrounded by birdsong. As the religious scholar Mary Evelyn Tucker says, "We belong here."

If we follow the logic of Lightman as I understand it, by abandoning the notion of reciprocity and acting as though "we have only ourselves to protect" we are agreeing to live selfishly, mindlessly, greedily at a terrible cost to the rest of our fellow inhabitants of the Earth Community. We adopt a solipsistic existence over a compassionate one.

Can't we acknowledge the glorious indifference of the natural world, and still engage in a reciprocal relationship with other beings? Part of being human is our capacity to hold seemingly opposing views in our mind at once. The Earth is wise with paradox.

Nature was not purposeless for Richard Jefferies, nor was his relationship with the Earth one-sided. It was reciprocal and alive and at the same time, he respected the Earth's sovereignty. "Nothing is consistent that is human," wrote Richard Jefferies.

If we are to survive as a species, we must also exercise a commitment toward the survival of other species, as well. Empathy becomes our story.

"Is there anything I can do?" he asks. "The mystery and the possibilities are not in the roots of the grass, nor is the depth of things in the sea; they are in my existence, in my soul." Jefferies goes on to say, "For want of words, I write soul, but I think it is beyond soul."

Could it be that the mind of the Earth is the cosmic mind as we witness the stellar eyes of galaxies burning down from the heavens? Our bodies and the bodies of stars are made from elemental fire. Each of us is married to the ongoing spiral of life. We live and we die and continue through the blades of grass that cover our graves.

Here a beautiful star shines clearly; here a constellation is hidden by a branch; a universe by a leaf.

The Story of My Heart written by Richard Jefferies reads like a prayer. *By prayer I do not mean a request for anything preferred to a deity; I mean intense soul-emotion, intense aspiration.* Isn't this what we house in our hearts, the emotions of our aspirations rising and falling like a flickering flame? I have never recognized my heart as a prayer chamber, until now.

Richard Jefferies felt the word deeply and dared to confront the Mysteries. He was relentless in his quest to name the ineffable. He was a lover of beauty. This is what we forget. Beauty is what opens our eyes to love. Love ignites passion and passion is what propels us toward the future wrought with risk and uncertainty. He was a man who lived with his eyes wide open.

"I lived in looking," Richard Jefferies said.

May we not avert our gaze.

THE STORY
OF MY HEART

by Richard Jefferies

Responses by Brooke Williams

CHAPTER I

~

The story of my heart commences seventeen years ago. In the glow of youth, there were times every now and then when I felt the necessity of a strong inspiration of soul-thought. My heart was dusty, parched for want of the rain of deep feeling; my mind arid and dry, for there is a dust, which settles on the heart as well as that which falls on a ledge. It is injurious to the mind as well as to the body to be always in one place and always surrounded by the same circumstances. A species of thick clothing slowly grows about the mind, the pores are choked, little habits become a part of existence, and by degrees the mind is inclosed in a husk. When this began to form, I felt eager to escape from it, to throw off the heavy clothing, to drink deeply once more at the fresh foundations of life. An inspiration—a long deep breath of the pure air of thought—could alone give health to the heart.

There is a hill to which I used to resort at such periods. The labour of walking three miles to it, all the while gradually ascending, seemed to clear my blood of the heaviness accumulated at home. On a warm summer day the slow continued rise required continual effort, which carried away the sense of oppression. The

familiar everyday scene was soon out of sight; I came
to other trees, meadows, and fields; I began to breathe
a new air and to have a fresher aspiration. I restrained
my soul till I reached the sward of the hill; psyche,
the soul that longed to be loose. I would write psyche
always instead of soul to avoid meanings which have
become attached to the word soul, but it is awkward
to do so. Clumsy indeed are all words, the moment the
wooden stage of commonplace life is left. I restrained
psyche, my soul, till I reached and put my foot on the
grass at the beginning of the green hill itself.

Moving up the sweet short turf, at every step my
heart seemed to obtain a wider horizon of feeling;
with every inhalation of rich pure air, a deeper desire.
The very light of the sun was whiter and more bril-
liant here. By the time I had reached the summit I had
entirely forgotten the petty circumstances and the an-
noyances of existence. I felt myself, myself. There was
an intrenchment on the summit, and going down into
the fosse I walked round it slowly to recover breath.
On the south-western side there was a spot where the
outer bank had partially slipped, leaving a gap. There
the view was over a broad plain, beautiful with wheat,
and inclosed by a perfect amphitheatre of green hills.
Through these hills there was one narrow groove, or
pass, southwards, where the white clouds seemed to
close in the horizon. Woods hid the scattered hamlets
and farmhouses, so that I was quite alone.

I was utterly alone with the sun and the earth.

Lying down on the grass, I spoke in my soul to the earth, the sun, the air, and the distant sea far beyond sight. I thought of the earth's firmness—I felt it bear me up: through the grassy couch there came an influence as if I could feel the great earth speaking to me. I thought of the wandering air—its pureness, which is its beauty; the air touched me and gave me something of itself. I spoke to the sea: though so far, in my mind I saw it, green at the rim of the earth and blue in deeper ocean; I desired to have its strength, its mystery and glory. Then I addressed the sun, desiring the soul equivalent of his light and brilliance, his endurance and unwearied race. I turned to the blue heaven over, gazing into its depth, inhaling its exquisite colour and sweetness. The rich blue of the unattainable flower of the sky drew my soul towards it, and there it rested, for pure colour is rest of heart. By all these I prayed; I felt an emotion of the soul beyond all definition; prayer is a puny thing to it, and the word is a rude sign to the feeling, but I know no other.

By the blue heaven, by the rolling sun bursting through untrodden space, a new ocean of ether every day unveiled. By the fresh and wandering air encompassing the world; by the sea sounding on the shore—the green sea white-flecked at the margin and the deep ocean; by the strong earth under me. Then, returning, I prayed by the sweet thyme, whose little flowers I touched with my hand; by the slender grass; by the crumble of dry chalky earth I took up and let fall through my fingers. Touching the crumble of earth, the blade of grass, the thyme flower, breathing the earth-encircling air, thinking of the sea and the sky, holding out my hand for the sunbeams to touch it, prone on the sward in token of deep reverence, thus I prayed that I might touch to the unutterable existence infinitely higher than deity.

With all the intensity of feeling which exalted me, all the intense communion I held with the earth, the sun and sky, the stars hidden by the light, with the ocean—in no manner can the thrilling depth of these feelings be written—with these I prayed, as if they were the keys of an instrument, of an organ, with which I swelled forth the note of my soul, redoubling my own voice by their power. The great sun burning with light; the strong earth, dear earth; the warm sky; the pure air; the thought of ocean; the inexpressible beauty of all filled me with a rapture, an ecstasy, and inflatus. With this inflatus, too, I prayed. Next to myself I came and recalled myself, my bodily existence. I held out my hand, the sunlight gleamed on the skin and the iridescent nails; I recalled the mystery and beauty of the flesh. I thought of the mind with which I could see the ocean sixty miles distant, and gather to myself its glory. I thought of my inner existence, that consciousness which is called the soul. These, that is, myself—I threw into the balance to weight the prayer the heavier. My strength of body, mind and soul, I flung into it; I put forth my strength; I wrestled and laboured, and toiled in might of prayer. The prayer, this soul-emotion was in itself not for an object—it was a passion. I hid my face in the grass, I was wholly prostrated, I lost myself in the wrestle, I was rapt and carried away.

Becoming calmer, I returned to myself and thought, reclining in rapt thought, full of aspiration, steeped to the lips of my soul in desire. I did not then define, or analyse, or understand this. I see now that what I laboured for was soul-life, more soul-nature, to be exalted, to be full of soul-learning. Finally I rose, walked half a mile or so along the summit of the hill eastwards, to soothe myself and come to the common ways of life again. Had any shepherd accidentally seen me lying on the turf, he would only have thought that I was resting a few minutes; I made no outward show. Who could have imagined the whirlwind of passion that was going on within me as I reclined there! I was greatly exhausted when I reached home. Occasionally I went upon the hill deliberately, deeming it good to do so; then, again, this craving carried me away up there of itself. Though the principal feeling was the same, there were variations in the mode in which it affected me.

Sometimes on lying down on the sward I first looked up at the sky, gazing for a long time till I could see deep into the azure and my eyes were full of the colour; then I turned my face to the grass and thyme, placing my hands at each side of my face so as to shut

out everything and hide myself. Having drunk deeply
of the heaven above and felt the most glorious beauty
of the day, and remembering the old, old, sea, which
(as it seemed to me) was but just yonder at the edge, I
now became lost, and absorbed into the being or existence of the universe. I felt down deep into the earth
under, and high above into the sky, and farther still to
the sun and stars. Still farther beyond the stars into
the hollow of space, and losing thus my separateness
of being came to seem like a part of the whole. Then I
whispered to the earth beneath, through the grass and
thyme, down into the depth of its ear, and again up to
the starry space hid behind the blue of day. Travelling
in an instant across the distant sea, I saw as if with actual vision the palms and cocoanut trees, the bamboos
of India, and the cedars of the extreme south. Like a
lake with islands the ocean lay before me, as clear and
vivid as the plain beneath in the midst of the amphitheatre of hills.

With the glory of the great sea, I said, with the
firm, solid, and sustaining earth; the depth, distance,
and expanse of ether; the age, tamelessness, and ceaseless motion of the ocean; the stars, and the unknown
in space; by all those things which are most powerful
known to me, and by those which exist, but of which I
have no idea whatever, I pray. Further, by my own soul,
that secret existence which above all other things bears
the nearest resemblance to the ideal of spirit, infinitely
nearer than earth, sun, or star. Speaking by an inclina-

tion towards, not in words, my soul prays that I may have something from each of these, that I may gather a flower from them, that I may have in myself the secret and meaning of the earth, the golden sun, the light, the foam-flecked sea. Let my soul become enlarged; I am not enough; I am little and contemptible. I desire a great-ness of soul, an irradiance of mind, a deeper insight, a broader hope. Give me power of soul, so that I may actually effect by its will that which I strive for.

In winter, though I could not then rest on the grass, or stay long enough to form any definite expression, I still went up to the hill once now and then, for it seemed that to merely visit the spot repeated all that I had previously said. But it was not only then.

In summer I went out into the fields, and let my soul inspire these thoughts under the trees, standing against the trunk, or looking up through the branches at the sky. If trees could speak, hundreds of them would say that I had had these soul-emotions under them. Leaning against the oak's massive trunk, and feeling the rough bark and the lichen at my back, looking southwards over the grassy fields, cowslip-yellow, at the woods on the slope, I thought my desire of deeper soul-life. Or under the green firs, looking upwards, the sky was more deeply blue at their tops; then the brake fern was unrolling, the doves cooing, the thickets astir, the late ash-leaves coming forth. Under the shapely rounded elms, by the hawthorn bushes and hazel, everywhere the same deep desire for the soul-nature; to have from all green things and from the sunlight the inner meaning which was not known to them, that I might be full of light as the woods of the sun's rays. Just to touch the lichened bark of a tree, or the end of a spray projecting over the path as I walked, seemed to repeat the same prayer in me.

The long-lived summer days dried and warmed the turf in the meadows. I used to lie down in solitary corners at full length on my back, so as to feel the embrace of the earth. The grass stood high above me, and the shadows of the tree branches danced on my face. I looked up at the sky, with half-closed eyes to bear the dazzling light. Bees buzzed over me, sometimes a butterfly passed, there was a hum in the air, greenfinches sang in the hedge. Gradually entering into the intense life of the summer days—a life which burned around as if every grass blade and leaf were a torch—I came to feel the long-drawn life of the earth back into the dimmest past, while the sun of the moment was warm on me. Sesostris on the most ancient sands of the south, in ancient, ancient days, was conscious of himself and of the sun. This sunlight linked me through the ages to that past consciousness. From all the ages my soul desired to take that soul-life which had flowed through them as the sunbeams had continually poured on earth. As the hot sands take up the heat, so would I take up that soul-energy. Dreamy in appearance, I was breathing full of existence; I was aware of the grass blades, the flowers, the leaves on hawthorn and tree. I seemed to live more largely through them, as if each were a pore through which I drank. The grasshoppers called and leaped, the greenfinches sang, the blackbirds happily fluted, all the air hummed with life. I was plunged deep in existence, and with all that existence, I prayed.

Through every grass blade in the thousand, thousand grasses; through the million leaves, veined and edge-cut, on bush and tree; through the song-notes and the marked feathers of the birds; through the insects' hum and the colour of the butterflies; through the soft warm air, the flecks of clouds dissolving—I used them all for prayer. With all the energy the sunbeams had poured unwearied on the earth since Sesostris was conscious of them on the ancient sands; with all the life that had been lived by vigorous man and beauteous woman since first in dearest Greece the dream of the gods was woven; with all the soul-life that had flowed a long stream down to me, I prayed that I might have a soul more than equal to, far beyond my conception of, these things of the past, the present, and the fullness of all life. Not only equal to these, but beyond, higher, and more powerful than I could imagine. That I might take from all their energy, grandeur, and beauty, and gather it into me. That my soul might be more than the cosmos of life.

I prayed with the glowing clouds of sunset and the soft light of the first star coming through the violet sky. At night with the stars, according to the season:

now with the Pleiades, now with the Swan or burning Sirius, and broad Orion's whole constellation, red Aldebaran, Arcturus, and the Northern Crown; with the morning star, the light-bringer, once now and then when I saw it, a white-gold ball in the violet-purple sky, or framed about with pale summer vapour floating away as red streaks shot horizontally in the east. A diffused saffron ascended into the luminous upper azure. The disk of the sun rose over the hill, fluctuating with throbs of light; his chest heaved in fervour of brilliance. All the glory of the sunrise filled me with broader and furnace-like vehemence of prayer. That I might have the deepest of soul-life, the deepest of all, deeper far than all this greatness of the visible universe and even of the invisible; that I might have a fullness of soul till now unknown, and utterly beyond my own conception.

In the deepest darkness of the night, the same thought rose in my mind as in the bright light of noontide. What is there which I have not used to strengthen the same emotion?

SYNCHRONICITY

Three years have passed since discovering this small book in that shop on the Maine Coast. We've read it many times. We've read what others have written about it. We've followed Richard Jefferies through the part of England where he was born and lived. We sat at the desk where he wrote, and looked out over the same landscape. And we walked some of the same paths he walked nearly every day of his life. I've reconstructed the history of my relationship with *The Story of My Heart*, and have a good idea *how* he managed to hijack my attention and then hold onto it this long. The more I learn about Richard Jefferies, the more I wonder *why*.

Terry started reading out loud. We were sitting on a rocky beach on the Maine Coast, perched against giant, pink granite boulders separating the forest from the sea. The autumn afternoon sun beat down on our shoulders and legs. On page one of *The Story of My Heart*, I heard the perfect combination of words: "An inspiration—a long deep breath of the pure air of thought," a promise of new expansive ideas that would challenge some of my beliefs and support others.

Finding Jefferies was the latest marker along a path I'd been following for three decades, since discovering that a different life existed beyond the "work for the man till you're 65"—suppress your passions—loyal

Mormon life I'd been given.

Terry and I met at a fork in my path—one paved and lit, complete with a secure job selling plumbing supplies, with "eternal life" guaranteed. The other was overgrown and wild and seemed difficult to follow, with no obvious goal. I'm not sure I could have negotiated this unpredictable, "road less travelled" alone. Knowing we could explore that unknown path together gave us courage.

Meeting Terry meant meeting her grandmother, Kathryn— "Mimi," we called her. Mimi had an insatiable appetite for knowledge and had accumulated an amazing library by some of the world's great thinkers. When Terry was five, Mimi first took her bird watching. They danced and painted and explored. Mimi fostered in Terry a clear sense of her own uniqueness that no one could challenge.

I, on the other hand, struggled.

I've struggled, knowing I play a role in our long-term ability to thrive on this blue spinning orb we call Earth, but pulled by a constant force toward the life modern men are supposed to live. Mimi left me her library when she died. These books by Carl G. Jung, Marie-Louise von Franz, J. Krishnamurti, Alan Watts, Ira Progoff, Joseph Campbell, and others have helped me understand my greater role in the world. I am not alone.

If page one of *The Story of My Heart* got my attention, page two captivated me. Jefferies writes:

I would write psyche always instead of soul to avoid meanings which have become attached to the word soul, but it is awkward to do so.

Jefferies was in conversation with me as I was in conversation with Jung. Jung also used "soul" and "psyche" interchangeably. The psyche, I've learned, is the complete human mind—conscious as well as unconscious. What intrigues me most is Jung's idea of the *collective unconscious*—that part of the psyche every human shares, that evolved as our cells evolved, through natural selection, consisting of "mnemonic deposits accruing from the experience of our ancestors."

Randomly discovering a book I'd never heard of and reading a passage about psyche and soul—concepts I'd been struggling to understand—was for me a "meaningful coincidence," Jung's definition for *synchronicity*.

Synchronicity is, according to Ira Progroff, "at the frontal edge of life where evolution is occurring."

As Terry and I read to each other that afternoon, the tide coming in, I couldn't believe we'd never heard of this man. If the dead are still out there among us in different form, and if Jefferies wanted to send me a message, he could not have sent more obvious clues. I felt as if I'd found a kindred spirit. We are part of the same story.

This story is about living in this modern world, vastly different from the natural world we evolved to live in. It's about the joy and peace and motivation we get from rediscovering that original world still alive in the remaining wild places. Jefferies writes less specifically about the natural world surrounding him, but in great detail the path his mind takes through that original world.

In Chapter I, Jefferies describes his pure experience, expecting the reader to make sense of his mystical euphoria. I would learn later how well-read Jefferies was despite being relatively uneducated. His confidence in relying on nothing outside of his own direct experience, something I need to learn.

Although separated in time by a century, Jefferies and Paul Shepard, one of my intellectual heroes, would have had a great conversation. Shepard suggests that we are made of an original, evolved core now covered by the veneer of civilization. Jefferies writes:

> A species of thick clothing slowly grows about the mind, the pores are choked, little habits become a part of existence, and by degrees the mind is enclosed in a husk. When this began to form I felt eager to escape from it, to throw off the heavy clothing, to drink deeply once more at the fresh foundations of life.

Later in Chapter I, Jefferies describes what happens to him lying on the grass on the side of a familiar hill, a three-mile walk from his house. While hearing Terry read this, I swear I heard Abraham Maslow describing a "peak experience." His book, *Religions, Values, and Peak Experiences*, consists of the information he got by asking over two thousand people to describe their "ecstasies, raptures…the most blissful and perfect moments of life."

Years ago, when I first read this book, I realized much of what I felt in the wild made sense far beyond my own considerations. Although nothing in my upbringing could accommodate these feelings, Maslow helped ground me in a different kind of truth, in a "hierarchy of needs" and what it means to be human— to be fed and safe, to dream. Many of the moments Jefferies describes from the hillside correspond perfectly to the elements Maslow uses to describe a peak experience.

For example: Maslow discovered that a person having a peak experience perceives the entire universe as an integrated whole, where they belong, in which they play an integral part. Jefferies writes about feeling integrated into the entire universe, "losing thus my separateness of being came to seem like a part of the whole."

Maslow suggests that people who have had a peak experience are no longer interested in organized religions, which are based on believing in the experience of someone else (Jesus, Mohammed, Buddha). Having a personal, primary, *peak* experience makes believing in a secondary experience difficult. This is a key element in Jefferies' life. Jefferies knew something else was out there and wanted desperately to experience "the unutterable existence infinitely *higher than deity.*"

By "deity" I think Jefferies is referring to the "God" he grew up with and was expected to believe in, a god too small and limited to fit into his personal experience. I know that feeling. I wonder if Abraham Maslow read anything by Richard Jefferies?

Each time I read Jefferies, I find more I relate to, more to justify the time and energy I've spent thinking about an obscure, nature-writing "mystic" who lived in England and died a century ago. I'm still searching for *why* Richard Jefferies matters, and what I'm supposed to do with that knowledge once I find it.

The Story of My Heart has been reissued many times since it was first published in 1883. New versions are published with new introductions by people who happened to believe that Jefferies had written something just for them. This volume is no exception. Classic works of literature need to be rediscovered and reinterpreted every age for their clues to contemporary issues. We are living in unique times—we've never been here before. Climate scientists tell us the next decade may be the most important in the history of our species. I believe *The Story of My Heart* has something to offer us, now.

As Terry read these passages, her back against boulders barely beyond the reach of high tide, a slight breeze swirled between us, scented with both pine and sea. We felt Jefferies' use of personal pronouns split open as they became our own.

CHAPTER II

~

S ometimes I went to a deep, narrow valley in the hills, silent and solitary. The sky crossed from side to side, like a roof supported on two walls of green. Sparrows chirped in the wheat at the verge above, their calls falling like the twittering of swallows from the air. There was no other sound. The short grass was dried grey as it grew by the heat; the sun hung over the narrow vale as if it had been put there by hand. Burning, burning, the sun glowed on the sward at the foot of the slope where these thoughts burned into me. How many, many years, how many cycles of years, how many bundles of cycles of years, had the sun glowed down thus on that hollow? Since it was formed how long? Since it was worn and shaped, groove-like, in the flanks of the hills by mighty forces which had ebbed. Alone with the sun which glowed on the work when it was done, I saw back through space to the old time of tree-ferns, of the lizard flying through the air, the lizard-dragon wallowing in sea foam, the mountainous creatures, twice-elephantine, feeding on land; all the crooked sequence of life. The dragonfly which passed me traced a continuous descent from the fly marked on stone in those days. The immense time lifted me like a wave rolling under a boat; my mind seemed to raise itself as the swell of the cycles came; it felt strong with the power of the ages. With all that time and power I prayed: that I might have in my soul the intellectual part of it; the idea, the thought. Like a shuttle the mind shot to and fro the past and the present, in an instant.

Full to the brim of the wondrous past, I felt the wondrous present. For the day—the very moment I breathed, that second of time then in the valley, was as marvellous, as grand, as all that had gone before. Now, this moment was the wonder and the glory. Now, this moment was exceedingly wonderful. Now, this moment give me all the thought, all the idea, all the soul expressed in the cosmos around me. Give me still more, for the interminable universe, past and present, is but earth; give me the unknown soul, wholly apart from it, the soul of which I know only that when I touch the ground, when the sunlight touches my hand, it is not there. Therefore the heart looks into space to be away from earth. With all the cycles, and the sunlight streaming through them, with all that is meant by the present, I thought in the deep vale and prayed.

There was a secluded spring to which I sometimes went to drink the pure water, lifting it in the hollow of my hand. Drinking the lucid water, clear as light itself in solution, I absorbed the beauty and purity of it. I drank the thought of the element; I desired soul-nature pure and limpid. When I saw the sparkling dew on the grass—a rainbow broken into drops—it called up the same thought-prayer. The stormy wind whose sudden twists laid the trees on the ground woke the same feeling; my heart shouted with it. The soft summer air which entered when I opened my window in the morning breathed the same sweet desire. At night, before sleeping, I always looked out at the shadowy trees, the hills looming indistinctly in the dark, a star seen between the drifting clouds; prayer of soul-life always. I chose the highest room, bare and gaunt, because as I sat at work I could look out and see more of the wide earth, more of the dome of the sky, and could think my desire through these. When the crescent of the new moon shone, all the old thoughts were renewed.

All the succeeding incidents of the year repeated my prayer as I noted them. The first green leaf on the hawthorn, the first spike of meadow grass, the first song of the nightingale, the green ear of wheat. I spoke it with the ear of wheat as the sun tinted it golden; with the whitening barley; again with the red gold spots of autumn on the beech, the buff oak leaves, and the gossamer dew-weighted. All the larks over the green corn sang it for me, all the dear swallows; the green leaves rustled it; the green brook flags waved it; the swallows took it with them to repeat it for me in distant lands. By the running brook I meditated it; a flash of sunlight here in the curve, a flicker yonder on the ripples, the birds bathing in the sandy shallow, the rush of falling water. As the brook ran winding through the meadow, so one thought ran winding through my days.

The sciences I studied never checked it for a moment; nor did the books of old philosophy. The sun was stronger than science; the hills more than philosophy. Twice circumstances gave me a brief view of the sea then the passion rose tumultuous as the waves. It was very bitter to me to leave the sea.

Sometimes I spent the whole day walking over the hills searching for it; as if the labour of walking would force it from the ground. I remained in the woods for hours, among the ash sprays and the fluttering of the ring-doves at their nests, the scent of pines here and there, dreaming my prayer.

My work was most uncongenial and useless, but even then sometimes a gleam of sunlight on the wall, the buzz of a bee at the window, would bring the thought to me. Only to make me miserable, for it was a waste of golden time while the rich sunlight streamed on hill and plain. There was a wrenching of the mind, a straining of the mental sinews; I was forced to do this, my mind was yonder. Weariness, exhaustion, nerve-illness often ensued. The insults which are showered on poverty, long struggle of labour, the heavy pressure of circumstances, the unhappiness, only stayed the expression of the feeling. It was always there. Often in the streets of London, as the red sunset flamed over the houses, the old thought, the old prayer, came.

Not only in grassy fields with green leaf and

running brook did this constant desire find renewal. More deeply still with living human beauty; the perfection of form, the simple fact of form, ravished and always will ravish me away. In this lies the outcome and end of all the loveliness of sunshine and green leaf, of flowers, pure water, and sweet air. This is embodiment and highest expression; the scattered, uncertain, and designless loveliness of tree and sunlight brought to shape. Through this beauty I prayed deepest and longest, and down to this hour. The shape—the divine idea of that shape—the swelling muscle or the dreamy limb, strong sinew or curve of bust, Aphrodite or Hercules, it is the same. That I may have the soul-life, the soul-nature, let divine beauty bring to me divine soul. Swart Nubian, white Greek, delicate Italian, massive Scandinavian, in all the exquisite pleasure the form gave, and gives, to me immediately becomes intense prayer.

If I could have been in physical shape like these, how despicable in comparison I am; to be shapely of form is so infinitely beyond wealth, power, fame, all that ambition can give, that these are dust before it. Unless of the human form, no pictures hold me; the rest are flat surfaces. So, too, with the other arts, they are dead; the potters, the architects, meaningless, stony, and some repellent, like the cold touch of porcelain. No prayer with these. Only the human form in art could raise it, and most in statuary. I have seen so little good statuary, it is a regret to me; still, that I have is beyond all other art. Fragments here, a bust yonder, the broken pieces brought from Greece, copies, plaster casts, a memory of an Aphrodite, of a Persephone, of an Apollo, that is all; but even drawings of statuary will raise the prayer. These statues were like myself full of a thought, for ever about to burst forth as a bud, yet silent in the same attitude. Give me to live the soul-life they express. The smallest fragment of marble carved in the shape of the human arm will wake the desire I felt in my hill-prayer.

Time went on; good fortune and success never for an instant deceived me that they were in themselves to be sought; only my soul-thought was worthy. Further years bringing much suffering, grinding the very life out; new troubles, renewed insults, loss of what hard labour had earned, the bitter question: Is it not better to leap into the sea? These, too, have made no impression; constant still to the former prayer my mind endures. It was my chief regret that I had not endeavoured to write these things, to give expression to this passion. I am now trying, but I see that I shall only in part succeed.

The same prayer comes to me at this very hour. It is now less solely associated with the sun and sea, hills, woods, or beauteous human shape. It is always within. It requires no waking; no renewal; it is always with me. I am it; the fact of my existence expresses it.

After a long interval, I came to the hills again, this time by the coast. I found a deep hollow on the side of a great hill, a green concave opening to the sea, where I could rest and think in perfect quiet. Behind me were furze bushes dried by the heat; immediately in front dropped the steep descent of the bowl-like hollow which received and brought up to me the faint sound of the summer waves. Yonder lay the immense plain of sea, the palest green under the continued sunshine, as though the heat had evaporated the colour from it; there was no distinct horizon, a heat-mist inclosed it and looked farther away than the horizon would have done. Silence and sunshine, sea and hill gradually brought my mind into the condition of intense prayer. Day after day, for hours at a time, I came there, my soul-desire always the same. Presently I began to consider how I could put a part of that prayer into form, giving it an object. Could I bring it into such a shape as would admit of actually working upon the lines it indicated for any good?

One evening, when the bright white star in Lyra was shining almost at the zenith over me, and the deep concave was the more profound in the dusk, I formulated it into three divisions. First, I desired that I might do or find something to exalt the soul, something to enable it to live its own life, a more powerful existence now. Secondly, I desired to be able to do something for the flesh, to make a discovery or perfect a method by which the fleshly body might enjoy more pleasure, longer life, and suffer less pain. Thirdly, to construct a more flexible engine with which to carry into execution the design of the will. I called this the Lyra prayer, to distinguish it from the far deeper emotion in which the soul was alone concerned.

Of the three divisions, the last was of so little importance that it scarcely deserved to be named in conjunction with the others. Mechanism increases convenience—in no degree does it confer physical or moral perfection. The rudimentary engines employed thousands of years ago in raising buildings were in that respect equal to the complicated machines of the present day. Control of iron and steel has not altered or improved the bodily man. I even debated some time whether such a third division should be included at all. Our bodies are now conveyed all round the world with ease, but obtain no advantage. As they start so they return. The most perfect human families of ancient times were almost stationary, as those of Greece. Perfection of form was found in Sparta; how small a spot compared to those continents over which we are now taken so quickly! Such perfection of form might perhaps again dwell, contented and complete in itself, on such a strip of land as I could see between me and the sand of the sea. Again, a watch keeping correct time is no guarantee that the bearer shall not suffer pain. The owner of the watch may be soulless, without mind-fire, a mere creature. No benefit to the heart or to the body accrues from the most accurate mechanism. Hence I debated whether the third division should be included. But I reflected that time cannot be put back on the dial, we cannot return to Sparta; there is an existent state of things, and existent multitudes; and possibly a more powerful engine, flexible to the will, might give them that freedom which is the one, and the one only, political or social idea I possess. For liberty, therefore, let it be included.

For the flesh, this arm of mine, the limbs of others gracefully moving, let me find something that will give them greater perfection. That the bones may be firmer, somewhat larger if that would be an advantage, certainly stronger, that the cartilage and sinews may be more enduring, and the muscles more powerful, something after the manner of those ideal limbs and muscles sculptured of old, these in the flesh and real. That the organs of the body may be stronger in their action, perfect, and lasting. That the exterior flesh may be yet more beautiful; that the shape may be finer, and the motions graceful. These are the soberest words I can find, purposely chosen; for I am so rapt in the beauty of the human form, and so earnestly, so inexpressibly, prayerful to see that form perfect, that my full thought is not to be written. Unable to express it fully, I have considered it best to put it in the simplest manner of words. I believe in the human form; let me find something, some method, by which that form may achieve the utmost beauty. Its beauty is like an arrow, which may be shot any distance according to the strength of the bow. So the idea expressed in the human shape is capable of indefinite expansion and elevation of beauty.

Of the mind, the inner consciousness, the soul, my prayer desired that I might discover a mode of life for it, so that it might not only conceive of such a life, but actually enjoy it on the earth. I wished to search out a new and higher set of ideas on which the mind should work. The simile of a new book of the soul is the nearest to convey the meaning—a book drawn from the present and future, not the past. Instead of a set of ideas based on tradition, let me give the mind a new thought drawn straight from the wondrous present, direct this very hour. Next, to furnish the soul with the means of executing its will, of carrying thought into action. In other words, for the soul to become a power. These three formed the Lyra prayer, of which the two first are immeasurably the more important. I believe in the human being, mind and flesh; form and soul.

It happened just afterwards that I went to Pevensey, and immediately the ancient wall swept my mind back seventeen hundred years to the eagle, the pilum, and the short sword. The grey stones, the thin red bricks laid by those whose eyes had seen Caesar's Rome, lifted me out of the grasp of house-life, of modern civilisation, of those minutiae which occupy the moment. The grey stone made me feel as if I had existed from then till now, so strongly did I enter into and see my own life as if reflected. My own existence was focused back on me; I saw its joy, its unhappiness, its birth, its death, its possibilities among the infinite, above all its yearning Question. Why? Seeing it thus clearly, and lifted out of the moment by the force of seventeen centuries, I recognised the full mystery and the depths of things in the roots of the dry grass on the wall, in the green sea flowing near. Is there anything I can do? The mystery and the possibilities are not in the roots of the grass, nor is the depth of things in the sea; they are in my existence, in my soul. The marvel of existence, almost the terror of it, was flung on me with crushing force by the sea, the sun shining, the distant hills. With all their ponderous weight they made me feel myself: all the time, all the centuries made me feel myself this moment a hundred-fold. I determined that I would endeavour to write what I had so long thought of, and the same evening put down one sentence. There the sentence remained two years. I tried to carry it on; I hesitated because I could not express it: nor can I now, though in desperation I am throwing these rude stones of thought together, rude as those of the ancient wall.

BODY

For Jefferies, the human form is nature at its zenith. He wrote this chapter suffering from tuberculosis, the illness that would kill him a few years later.
"How despicable in comparison I am" to "Swart Nubian, white Greek, delicate Italian, massive Scandinavian." How devastating it must have been for this
rigorous man to have been nearly bedridden for the
last four years of his life. Jefferies was known to keep
a strict schedule that included walking eight to ten
miles every day.

He loved the human form and loved the statues
that captured it, particularly those carved in marble
from Greece. "The smallest fragment of marble carved
in the shape of an arm will wake the desire I felt in my
hill-prayer." Sparta, the ancient city-state in Greece,
was the standard of perfection for Jefferies, where "the
most perfect human families" lived.

I had some sense of the Spartans, but not much.
The film *300*, about Spartan warriors, was played by
actors with perfect bodies. To achieve this level of fit-
ness, they trained day and night for months in Salt
Lake City with Mark Twight at Gym Jones. Although
I never trained at Gym Jones, I frequented Mountain
Athlete in Jackson Hole, where I was coached by Rob
Shaul, whom Twight inspired and mentored. While I
didn't reach the physical beauty that so enamored Jef-

feries (nor did I look anything like the actors in *300*) I was in the best shape of my life. This made me wonder about the ideal human form, and whether it actually exists. "Evolutionary exercise" is the philosophy that the ideal fitness program should mimic as closely as possible the life humans evolved to live. Art De Vany, the man who coined the term, wrote about what our bodies are built to do.

> A historical source reports that five Indian braves drove five bison into a pit. After they killed these two-thousand-pound bison, they pulled them out of a pit more than ten feet deep, lined them up and skinned and butchered them. Then, they carried as much as they could back to camp to get others to return for the rest.

We have grown soft in terms of what most of us ask of our bodies. Spartan bodies are sculpted in gyms, not earned in the wilds through the work of survival.

Jefferies acknowledges that "we cannot return to Sparta" but wonders about physical perfection as "capable of indefinite expansion and elevation of beauty."

"Nature in the Louvre," one of the last essays Jefferies wrote, is an ode to the beauty found in classic Greek and Roman statues.

Terry and I decided in order to truly understand and appreciate the words of Richard Jefferies, we had to experience the Wilshire landscape that inspired him. We needed to wander along his paths and look out over the same vistas he did during his daily walks.

Planning our trip, I thought about the word "vacation" and couldn't remember having one. Terry and I have travelled—but always in search of something, on a quest. After working at the Teton Science School in Jackson Hole when we were first married, we travelled to Alaska to get a sense of this massive northern landscape that had shaped the lives of the Muries: Olaus and Mardy, Adolph and Louise. We could have never imagined the richness and romance we found in Spain while researching Terry's book *Leap*. We explored the deepest corners of Southern Utah working on wilderness issues. And islands—Maui to visit friends Paula and her husband, the poet W.S. Merwin; one thousand miles south of Hawaii to Palmyra to write for the Nature Conservancy; Antelope and Fremont Islands in Great Salt Lake with students. We went to the Galapagos in the footsteps of Charles Darwin, one of my heroes. Hell, we came home from Rwanda with Louis, who would become our son. The logistics of following Jefferies to Europe were simple, straightforward. We knew where to go and how to get there. What we didn't know exactly was *why*, which makes all the difference.

We started with an excursion to Paris, in hopes of exploring Jefferies' imagination. Our first stop was the Louvre. We would use "Nature in the Louvre" as a guide.

The entire essay, it turns out, focuses on one Greek statue: *Venus Accroupie* or the *Crouching Venus*. Richard

Jefferies was obsessed with this statue of a crouching woman. She was missing her head and hands. The small hand in the middle of her back once belonged to a child she carried. Jefferies visited this statue and this statue only on at least three different days.

I'd been to the Louvre twice before and tried to retrace my steps, wondering if I'd seen her. In truth, I couldn't remember. Jefferies describes the hordes of people walking straight past *Accroupie*, without so much as a casual glance, on their way to *Venus de Milo*. I was one of them, hurrying with map in hand through the long hall filled with pinkish-white Greek and Roman statues, glancing left and right, thinking that time had been tough on men's genitalia, wondering if there was anything we should be learning from that visual fact.

Before we entered the Louvre in search of Jefferies' beloved, we read:

> The right arm looks as if it had passed partly under the left breast, the fingers resting on the left knee, which is raised; while the left arm was uplifted to maintain the balance. The shoulders are massive rather than broad, and do not overshadow the width of the hips. The right knee is rounded, because it is bent; the left knee less so, because raised. Bending the right knee has the effect of slightly widening the right thigh. The right knee is very noble, bold in its slow curve, strong and beautiful.

Jefferies writes about joints and grooves and folds of skin and how real *Accroupie* seems compared to *de Milo*, who has no joints or grooves. At first, while reading about breasts and "hovering lines" and flesh "drawn tightly against the firm structure under the skin," I began to think Jefferies had a prurient view of the female form, which, I admit, had me wondering about his sex life. I looked up the term "mesial groove," wondering about the "flatness" at the lower end of the mesial groove that Jefferies referred to as, "somewhat in the shape of an elongated diamond; it is rather below the loins, and is, I think, caused by the commencement or upper part of the pelvis." Honestly, I was disappointed to learn that mesial groove describes simply the middle line of the body, which might say more about me than Jefferies.

Once inside the Louvre we found our way to *Ac-*

croupie and sat down on the bench facing her. For Jefferies, *Accroupie* was the ideal human—her strength and "Immense vitality of form," "not too feminine; with all her tenderness, she can think and act as nobly as a man." But most of all, he was touched by the balance of love emanating from her, and the way she "stoops to please the children, that they may climb on her back."

Terry saw through the stone, beyond the artist and the art. "Who was this woman who the artist used as a model?" she asked after sitting, watching quietly. "What happened to her child?" Terry asked, referring to the small hand on *Accroupie*'s back. We walked around her, just as Jefferies had done, looking at her from different angles and distances. I drew pictures of her in my notebook, including her folds and joints and

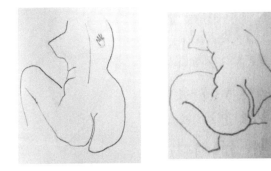

mesial grooves. I took photos of her. We spent the day with her, the changing light turning the marble translucent. I thought I saw her breathe.

To Jefferies, the ideal human body is wildness in tangible form. The *ideal* body is beautiful because it is the latest result of evolution. *Accroupie* reminded Jefferies of the "loveliness of nature…days which I had spent wandering among deep meadows and by green woods…"

Accroupie is a work of genius, which Jefferies differentiates from talent—"a hundred clever things," whereas genius "gives us but one example." I believe it is from the genius of wildness that the genius of Jefferies emerges, in the same way that the strong, elemental force possessed by this statue moved him.

reasons, whether the soul lives on or not, I am fully aware. I do not hope or fear. At least while I am living I have enjoyed the idea of immortality, and the idea of my own soul. If then, after death, I am resolved without exception into earth, air, and water, and the spirit goes out like a flame, still I shall have had the glory of that thought.

It happened once that a man was drowned while bathing, and his body was placed in an outhouse near the garden. I passed the outhouse continually, sometimes on purpose to think about it, and it always seemed to me that the man was still living. Separation is not to be comprehended; the spirit of the man did not appear to have gone to an inconceivable distance. As my thought flashes itself back through the centuries to the luxury of Canopus, and can see the gilded couches of a city extinct, so it slips through the future, and immeasurable time in front is no boundary to it. Certainly the man was not dead to me.

Sweetly the summer air came up to the tumulus, the grass sighed softly, the butterflies went by, sometimes alighting on the green dome. Two thousand years! Summer after summer the blue butterflies had visited the mound, the thyme had flowered, the wind sighed in the grass. The azure morning had spread its arms over the low tomb; and full glowing noon burned on it; the purple of sunset rosied the sward. Stars, ruddy in the vapour of the southern horizon, beamed at midnight through the mystic summer night, which is dusky and yet full of light. White mists swept up and hid it; dews rested on the turf; tender harebells drooped; the wings of the finches fanned the air—finches whose colours faded from the wings how many centuries ago! Brown autumn dwelt in the woods beneath; the rime of winter whitened the beech clump on the ridge; again the buds came on the wind-blown hawthorn bushes, and in the evening the broad constellation of Orion covered the east. Two thousand times! Two thousand times the woods grew green, and ring-doves built their nests. Day and night for two thousand years—light and shadow sweeping over the mound—two thousand years of labour by day and slumber by night. Mystery gleaming in the stars, pouring down in the sunshine, speaking in the night, the wonder of the sun and of far space, for twenty centuries round about this low and green-grown dome. Yet all that mystery and wonder is as nothing to the Thought that lies therein, to the spirit that I feel so close.

Realising that spirit, recognising my own inner consciousness, the psyche, so clearly, I cannot understand time. It is eternity now. I am in the midst of it. It is about me in the sunshine; I am in it, as the butterfly floats in the light-laden air. Nothing has to come; it is now. Now is eternity; now is the immortal life. Here this moment, by this tumulus, on earth, now; I exist in it. The years, the centuries, the cycles are absolutely nothing; it is only a moment since this tumulus was raised; in a thousand years it will still be only a moment. To the soul there is no past and no future; all is and will be ever, in now. For artificial purposes time is mutually agreed on, but is really no such thing. The shadow goes on upon the dial, the index moves round upon the clock, and what is the difference? None whatever. If the clock had never been set going, what would have been the difference? There may be time for the clock, the clock may make time for itself; there is none for me.

I dip my hand in the brook and feel the stream; in an instant the particles of water which first touched me have floated yards down the current, my hand remains there. I take my hand away, and the flow—the time—of the brook does not exist to me. The great clock of the firmament, the sun and the stars, the crescent moon, the earth circling two thousand times, is no more to me than the flow of the brook when my hand is withdrawn; my soul has never been, and never can be, dipped in time. Time has never existed, and never will; it is a purely artificial arrangement. It is eternity now, it always was eternity, and always will be. By no possible means could I get into time if I tried. I am in eternity now and must there remain. Haste not, be at rest, this Now is eternity. Because the idea of time has left my mind—if ever it had any hold on it—to me the man interred in the tumulus is living now as I live. We are both in eternity.

There is no separation—no past; eternity, the

Now, is continuous. When all the stars have revolved
they only produce Now again. The continuity of Now
is forever. So that it appears to me purely natural,
and not super natural, that the soul whose temporary
frame was interred in this mound should be existing
as I sit on the sward. How infinitely deeper is thought
than the million miles of the firmament! The wonder
is here, not there; now, not to be, now always. Things
that have been miscalled supernatural appear to me
simple, more natural than nature, than earth, than sea,
or sun. It is beyond telling more natural that I should
have a soul than not, that there should be immortality; I think there is much more than immortality. It
is matter which is the supernatural, and difficult of
understanding. Why this clod of earth I hold in my
hand? Why this water which drops sparkling from
my fingers dipped in the brook? Why are they at all?
When? How? What for? Matter is beyond understanding, mysterious, impenetrable; I touch it easily, comprehend it, no. Soul, mind—the thought, the
idea—is easily understood, it understands itself and
is conscious.

The supernatural miscalled, the natural in truth,
is the real. To me everything is supernatural. How
strange that condition of mind, which cannot accept
anything but the earth, the sea, the tangible universe!
Without the misnamed supernatural these to me seem
incomplete, unfinished. Without soul all these are
dead. Except when I walk by the sea, and my soul is

If, when I die, that "I" also dies, and becomes extinct, still even then I have had the exaltation of these ideas.

How many words it has taken to describe so briefly the feelings and the thoughts that came to me by the tumulus; thoughts that swept past and were gone, and were succeeded by others while yet the shadow of the mound had not moved from one thyme flower to another, not the breadth of a grass blade. Softly breathed the sweet south wind, gently the yellow corn waved beneath; the ancient, ancient sun shone on the fresh grass and the flower, my heart opened wide as the broad, broad earth. I spread my arms out, laying them on the sward, seizing the grass, to take the fullness of the days. Could I have my own way after death I would be burned on a pyre of pine-wood, open to the air, and placed on the summit of the hills. Then let my ashes be scattered abroad—not collected in an urn—freely sown wide and broadcast. That is the natural interment of man—of man whose Thought at least has been among the immortals; interment in the elements. Burial is not enough, it does not give sufficient solution into the elements speedily; a furnace is confined. The high open air of the topmost hill, there let the tawny flame lick up the fragment called the body; there cast the ashes into the space it longed for while living. Such a luxury of interment is only for the wealthy; I fear I shall not be able to afford it. Else the smoke of my resolution into the elements should certainly arise in time on the hilltop.

The silky grass sighs as the wind comes carrying the blue butterfly more rapidly than his wings. A large humblebee burrs round the green dome against which I rest; my hands are scented with thyme. The sweetness of the day, the fullness of the earth, the beauteous earth, how shall I say it?

Three things only have been discovered of that which concerns the inner consciousness since before written history began. Three things only in twelve thousand written, or sculptured, years, and in the dumb, dim time before then. Three ideas the Cavemen primeval wrested from the unknown, the night which is round us still in daylight—the existence of the soul, immortality, the deity. These things found, prayer followed as a sequential result. Since then nothing further has been found in all the twelve thousand years, as if men had been satisfied and had found these to suffice. They do not suffice me. I desire to advance further, and to wrest a fourth, and even still more than a fourth, from the darkness of thought. I want more ideas of soul-life. I am certain that there are more yet to be found. A great life—an entire civilisation—lies just outside the pale of common thought. Cities and countries, inhabitants, intelligences, culture—an entire civilisation. Except by illustrations drawn from familiar things, there is no way of indicating a new idea. I do not mean actual cities, actual civilisation. Such life is different from any yet imagined. A nexus of ideas exists of which nothing is known—a vast system of ideas—a cosmos of thought. There is an Entity, a Soul-Entity, as yet unrecognised. These, rudely expressed, constitute my Fourth Idea. It is beyond, or beside, the three discovered by the Cavemen; it is in addition to the existence of the soul; in addition to immortality; and beyond the idea of the deity. I think there is something more than existence.

There is an immense ocean over which the mind can sail, upon which the vessel of thought has not yet been launched. I hope to launch it. The mind of so many thousand years has worked round and round inside the circle of these three ideas as a boat on an inland lake. Let us haul it over the belt of land, launch on the ocean, and sail outwards.

There is so much beyond all that has ever yet been imagined. As I write these words, in the very moment, I feel that the whole air, the sunshine out yonder lighting up the ploughed earth, the distant sky, the circumambient ether, and that far space, is full of soul-secrets, soul-life, things outside the experience of all the ages. The fact of my own existence as I write, as I exist at this second, is so marvellous, so miracle-like, strange, and supernatural to me, that I unhesitatingly conclude I am always on the margin of life illimitable, and that there are higher conditions than existence. Everything around is supernatural; everything so full of unexplained meaning.

Twelve thousand years since the Caveman stood at the mouth of his cavern and gazed out at the night and the stars. He looked again and saw the sun rise beyond the sea. He reposed in the noontide heat under the shade of the trees, he closed his eyes and looked into himself. He was face to face with the earth, the sun, the night; face to face with himself. There was nothing between; no wall of written tradition; no built up system of culture—his naked mind was confronted by naked earth. He made three idea-discoveries, wresting them from the unknown; the existence of his soul, immortality, the deity. Now, today, as I write, I stand in exactly the same position as the Caveman. Written tradition, systems of culture, modes of thought, have for me no existence. If ever they took any hold of my mind it must have been very slight; they have long ago been erased.

From earth and sea and sun, from night, the stars, from day, the trees, the hills, from my own soul—from these I think. I stand this moment at the mouth of the ancient cave, face to face with nature, face to face with the supernatural, with myself. My naked mind confronts the unknown. I see as clearly as the noonday that this is not all; I see other and higher conditions than existence; I see not only the existence of the soul, immortality, but, in addition, I realise a soul-life illimitable; I realise the existence of a cosmos of thought; I realise the existence of an inexpressible entity infinitely higher than deity. I strive to give utterance to a Fourth Idea. The very idea that there is another idea is something gained. The three found by the Cavemen are but stepping-stones: first links of an endless chain. At the mouth of the ancient cave, face to face with the unknown, they prayed. Prone in heart today I pray, Give me the deepest soul-life.

MYSTIC

In June of 1964, Mimi, Terry's grandmother, read *This is It*, by Alan Watts. I know because this book, like all of those she left to me when she died, has her name, address, phone number, and when she read it written in perfect cursive inside the front cover. She preferred red ballpoint pens to personalize and annotate her books, but in this one she used green and blue, and red to differentiate the times when she re-read parts of it. Watts, a British philosopher who brought eastern religions to western audiences, wrote *This is It: and Other Essays on Zen and Spiritual Experience* in 1958.

Recently, I came across *What Would You Do if Money Were No Object?* a lovely video featuring Watts' words and voice about how we're coerced into living meaningless lives. After watching it, I wanted to know more about Alan Watts. I found *This is It* on the shelves where we keep Mimi's library. I opened it to the first page and read:

> The most impressive fact in man's spiritual, intellectual, and poetic experience has always been, for me, the universal prevalence of those astonishing moments of insight which Richard Bucke called "cosmic consciousness."

With her blue pen, Mimi had underlined Bucke's name and in the right margin had written, as if directly to Terry and me, "This book again."

During our visit to the Richard Jefferies Museum near Swindon, England, I found *Cosmic Consciousness* by Richard Maurice Bucke in the museum library. I'd never heard of it before. First published in 1901, it has been called "one of the great classics of mystical experience." Bucke outlines the factors shared by people who like himself had attained what he calls "cosmic consciousness." Bucke includes Jesus, Plotinus, Buddha, Muhammad, Dante, William Blake, and Walt Whitman as examples of people who achieved cosmic consciousness. Later, Jefferies is listed with Moses, Isaiah, Socrates, Spinoza, Emerson, and Thoreau as having what Bucke calls "lesser, imperfect, or doubtful instances" of cosmic consciousness.

Cosmic consciousness consists of many elements—including the feeling of being immersed in a "rose-coloured cloud," experiencing joy, assurance, salvation, immortality, loss of fear of death or any sense of sin, and positive changes in appearance and personality. Moments of cosmic consciousness seem very similar to what Abraham Maslow later described as "peak experiences."

Of all the terms used to describe Richard Jefferies—from "sportsman," to "poet-naturalist," to "novelist"—"nature-mystic" intrigues me most. I think of mysticism as belonging to the occult, magical, and beyond the ability of science to grasp. I believe in the mystical and have had a few experiences that I can't describe logically, rationally. Mysteries, I believe, are part of life. I'm comfortable with this.

My first impulse was to assume that based on the mystical experiences he describes in *The Story of My Heart*, Jefferies had achieved cosmic consciousness. Not according to Bucke.

Bucke refers to passages in *The Story of My Heart*—many of them in Chapter III—as proof that Jefferies hadn't reached the pinnacle of cosmic consciousness. Bucke notes that Jefferies suffered a lack of confidence in his own ideas and suggests that Jefferies' love of nature "is always a longing, becoming intense but never fulfilled." Cosmically conscious individuals, according to Bucke, have made peace with death. For Jefferies, "death did not *seem*...to affect the personality..." Bucke writes. "He (Jefferies) has the feeling of continuous life—it does not *seem* that he can die. If he had attained Cosmic Consciousness he would have entered into eternal life, and there would be no 'seems' about it."

"I feel on the margin of a life unknown, very near, almost touching it," Jefferies writes, "on the verge of powers which, if I could grasp, would give me an immense breadth of existence."

And Bucke responds: "He feels that he has not realized—that there is something just out of reach: his contentment is never complete or only so by flashes... those who have entered Cosmic Consciousness...are at rest and happy." Bucke quotes Walt Whitman, the epitome of Cosmic Consciousness: "I know I am solid and sound…I know I am deathless."

This feels familiar. I'm constantly searching for meaning and truth, while for Terry, meaning and truth are part of the air she breathes. Mimi believed in reincarnation and often talked about people in terms of how many times they'd "been around"—are they open and receptive to new ideas, nurturing, and comfortable with mystery? Or is this their first time around—are they difficult, narcissistic, moody? Mimi said that Terry has "been around" many times. I know she's been around more than I have, but that this isn't my first time. There's real magic at play here.

Practically speaking, modern society insists that one of us keeps track of rule—where to park legally, taxes, oil changes, maps, etc.—so the other can focus on the real necessities: fresh flowers, art, silence, simplicity. Settling into a hotel room is a good example of this. First, she moves all the magazines and hotel information into a drawer, out of sight, and puts the small coffee maker in the closet. While she assembles her traveling altar (with location specific fetishes, feathers, small stones), I figure out how to unplug the small refrigerator to make it stop humming. She covers offensive art with a large shawl she carries. I leave to take a brisk walk, getting to know the neighborhood and find fresh flowers. I'm glad the soft drink machine and icemaker are on a different floor, as they can be difficult to dismantle.

Spiritually, I'm convinced that we're in each other's lives because somehow we both knew we needed one another to keep moving, growing. Put simply, I've been Terry's guide to a more expansive outer world, while she's led me deeper into the inner world.

Reading this chapter alongside Bucke's comments, I realized that lurking behind my eyes, back there in the shadows, is the feeling of how frustrated Jefferies must have been. I feel it in his prose, between the lines and in the margins. I don't think he was at peace in the sense that Whitman was. In *The Story of My Heart* he longs for something—he's not sure what. He writes about the three ideas of the caveman who had been buried near Jefferies' home two thousand years before: soul, immortality, the deity. These three ideas are no longer enough for him, and Jefferies longs for a fourth idea, yet to be known, that would lead to "A great life." This, Bucke suggests, is another example of "the Cosmic sense, which Jefferies felt but did not enter upon."

Jefferies, the mystic, could have sensed the possibility of a diminished and dangerous future like that a warming climate might be pushing us toward, which, to be avoided, would require a fourth idea. I wonder, had he lived more than his thirty-eight years, what Jefferies might have learned about the future from his continued time immersed in the natural world.

Mimi the mystic? Perhaps. Her mental ease as she moved through her life, my sense that she knew much more than she let on, and the comfort with which she faced her impending death, embodied a cosmic consciousness. Did she know the seeds she planted?

One hot evening years ago, Terry and I were floating in an eddy of the Colorado River preparing for the sunset. Just at the moment when even the air turned orange, a massive cloud of just-born mayflies exploded around us. We had mayflies in our eyes, hanging from our brows, mating in our hair. We couldn't breathe—we were drowning in mayflies. As quickly as it began, the moment ended and we rinsed their skins from our skin.

A moment of cosmic consciousness? Possibly. A peak experience? Perhaps. That experience shared elements of both. What we call it doesn't matter as no words come close to describing the hum that vibrated across my shoulders and down my back, reminding me that this moment was one of an infinite number of perfect moments occurring all around us, all of the time.

CHAPTER IV

~

The wind sighs through the grass, sighs in the sunshine; it has drifted the butterfly eastwards along the hill. A few yards away there lies the skull of a lamb on the turf, white and bleached, picked clean long since by crows and ants. Like the faint ripple of the summer sea sounding in the hollow of the ear, so the sweet air ripples in the grass. The ashes of the man interred in the tumulus are indistinguishable; they have sunk away like rain into the earth; so his body has disappeared. I am under no delusion; I am fully aware that no demonstration can be given of the three stepping-stones of the Cavemen. The soul is inscrutable; it is not in evidence to show that it exists; immortality is not tangible. Full well I know that reason and knowledge and experience tend to disprove all three; that experience denies answer to prayer. I am under no delusion whatever; I grasp death firmly in conception as I can grasp this bleached bone; utter extinction, annihilation. That the soul is a product at best of organic composition; that it goes out like a flame. This may be the end; my soul may sink like rain into the earth and disappear. Wind and earth, sea, and night and day, what then? Let my soul be but a product, what then? I say it is nothing to me;

this only I know, that while I have lived—now, this moment, while I live—I think immortality, I lift my mind to a Fourth Idea. If I pass into utter oblivion, yet I have had that.

The original three ideas of the Cavemen became encumbered with superstition; ritual grew up, and ceremony, and long ranks of souls were painted on papyri waiting to be weighed in the scales, and to be punished or rewarded. These cobwebs grotesque have sullied the original discoveries and cast them into discredit. Erase them altogether, and consider only the underlying principles. The principles do not go far enough, but I shall not discard all of them for that. Even supposing the pure principles to be illusions, and annihilation the end, even then it is better—it is something gained to have thought them. Thought is life; to have thought them is to have lived them. Accepting two of them as true in principle, then I say that these are but the threshold. For twelve thousand years no effort has been made to get beyond that threshold. These are but the primer of soul-life; the merest hieroglyphics chipped out, a little shape given to the unknown.

Not tomorrow but today. Not the tomorrow of the tumulus, the hour of the sunshine now. This moment give me to live soul-life, not only after death. Now is eternity, now I am in the midst of immortality; now the supernatural crowds around me. Open my mind, give my soul to see, let me live it now on earth, while I hear the burring of the larger bees, the sweet air in the grass, and watch the yellow wheat wave beneath me. Sun and earth and sea, night and day—these are the least of things. Give me soul-life.

There is nothing human in nature. The earth, though loved so dearly, would let me perish on the ground, and neither bring forth food nor water. Burning in the sky the great sun, of whose company I have been so fond, would merely burn on and make no motion to assist me. Those who have been in an open boat at sea without water have proved the mercies of the sun, and of the deity who did not give them one drop of rain, dying in misery under the same rays that smile so beautifully on the flowers. In the south the sun is the enemy; night and coolness and rain are the friends of man. As for the sea, it offers us salt water which we cannot drink. The trees care nothing for us; the hill I visited so often in days gone by has not missed me. The sun scorches man, and willing his naked state roast him alive. The sea and the fresh water alike make no effort to uphold him if his vessel founders; he casts up his arms in vain, they come to their level over his head, filling the spot his body occupied. If he falls from a cliff the air parts; the earth beneath dashes him to pieces.

Water he can drink, but it is not produced for him; how many thousands have perished for want of it? Some fruits are produced which he can eat, but they do not produce themselves for him; merely for the purpose of continuing their species. In wild, tropical countries, at the first glance there appears to be some consideration for him, but it is on the surface only. The lion pounces on him, the rhinoceros crushes him, the serpent bites, insects torture, diseases rack him. Disease worked its dreary will even among the flower-crowned Polynesians. Returning to our own country, this very thyme which scents my fingers did not grow for that purpose, but for its own. So does the wheat beneath; we utilise it, but its original and native purpose was for itself. By night it is the same as by day; the stars care not, they pursue their courses revolving, and we are nothing to them. There is nothing human in the whole round of nature. All nature, all the universe that we can see, is absolutely indifferent to us, and except to us human life is of no more value than grass. If the entire human race perished at this hour, what difference would it make to the earth? What would the earth care? As much as for the extinct dodo, or for the fate of the elephant now going.

On the contrary, a great part, perhaps the whole, of nature and of the universe is distinctly anti-human. The term inhuman does not express my meaning, anti-human is better; outre-human, in the sense of beyond, outside, almost grotesque in its attitude towards, would nearly convey it. Everything is anti-human. How extraordinary, strange, and incomprehensible are the creatures captured out of the depths of the sea! The distorted fishes; the ghastly cuttles; the hideous eel-like shapes; the crawling shell-encrusted things; the centipede-like beings; monstrous forms, to see which gives a shock to the brain. They shock the mind because they exhibit an absence of design. There is no idea in them.

They have no shape, form, grace, or purpose; they call up a vague sense of chaos, chaos which the mind revolts from. It would be a relief to the thought if they ceased to be, and utterly disappeared from the sea. They are not inimical of intent towards man, not even the shark; but there the shark is, and that is enough. These miserably hideous things of the sea are not anti-human in the sense of persecution, they are outside, they are ultra and beyond. It is like looking into chaos, and it is vivid because these creatures, interred alive a hundred fathoms deep, are seldom seen; so that the mind sees them as if only that moment they had come into existence. Use has not habituated it to them, so that their anti-human character is at once apparent, and stares at us with glassy eye.

But it is the same in reality with the creatures on the earth. There are some of these even now to which use has not accustomed the mind. Such, for instance, as the toad. At its shapeless shape appearing in an unexpected corner many people start and exclaim. They are aware that they shall receive no injury from it, yet it affrights them, it sends a shock to the mind. The reason lies in its obviously anti-human character. All the designless, formless chaos of chance-directed matter, without idea or human plan, squats there embodied in the pathway. By watching the creature, and convincing the mind from observation that it is harmless, and even has uses, the horror wears away. But still remains the form to which the mind can never reconcile itself. Carved in wood it is still repellent.

Or suddenly there is a rustle like a faint hiss in the grass, and a green snake glides over the bank. The breath in the chest seems to lose its vitality; for an instant the nerves refuse to transmit the force of life. The gliding yellow-streaked worm is so utterly opposed to the ever-present Idea in the mind. Custom may reduce the horror, but no long pondering can ever bring that creature within the pale of the human Idea. These are so distinctly opposite and anti-human that thousands of years have not sufficed to soften their outline. Various insects and creeping creatures excite the same sense in lesser degrees. Animals and birds in general do not. The tiger is dreaded, but causes no disgust. The exception is in those that feed on offal. Horses and dogs we love; we not only do not recognise anything opposite in them, we come to love them.

They are useful to us, they show more or less sympathy with us, they possess, especially the horse, a certain grace of movement. A gloss, as it were, is thrown over them by these attributes and by familiarity. The shape of the horse to the eye has become conventional: it is accepted. Yet the horse is not in any sense human. Could we look at it suddenly, without previous acquaintance, as at strange fishes in a tank, the ultra-human character of the horse would be apparent. It is the curves of the neck and body that carry the horse past without adverse comment. Examine the hind legs in detail, and the curious backward motion, the shape and anti-human curves become apparent. Dogs take us by their intelligence, but they have no hand; pass the hand over the dog's head, and the shape of the skull to the sense of feeling is almost as repellent as the form of the toad to the sense of sight. We have gradually gathered around us all the creatures that are less markedly anti-human, horses and dogs and birds, but they are still themselves. They originally existed like the wheat, for themselves; we utilise them, but they are not of us.

There is nothing human in any living animal. All nature, the universe as far as we see, is anti- or ultra-human, outside, and has no concern with man. These things are unnatural to him. By no course of reasoning, however tortuous, can nature and the universe be fitted to the mind. Nor can the mind be fitted to the cosmos. My mind cannot be twisted to it; I am separate altogether from these designless things. The soul cannot be wrested down to them. The laws of nature are of no importance to it. I refuse to be bound by the laws of the tides, nor am I so bound. Though bodily swung round on this rotating globe, my mind always remains in the centre. No tidal law, no rotation, no gravitation can control my thought.

Centuries of thought have failed to reconcile and

fit the mind to the universe, which is designless, and purposeless, and without idea. I will not endeavour to fit my thought to it any longer; I find and believe myself to be distinct—separate; and I will labour in earnest to obtain the highest culture for myself. As these natural things have no connection with man, it follows again that the natural is the strange and mysterious, and the supernatural the natural.

There being nothing human in nature or the universe, and all things being ultra-human and without design, shape, or purpose, I conclude that no deity has anything to do with nature. There is no god in nature, nor in any matter anywhere, either in the clods on the earth or in the composition of the stars. For what we understand by the deity is the purest form of Idea, of Mind, and no mind is exhibited in these. That which controls them is distinct altogether from deity. It is not force in the sense of electricity, nor a deity as god, nor a spirit, not even an intelligence, but a power quite different to anything yet imagined. I cease, therefore, to look for deity in nature or the cosmos at large, or to trace any marks of divine handiwork. I search for traces of this force which is not god, and is certainly not higher than the deity of whom I have written. It is a force without a mind. I wish to indicate something more subtle than electricity, but absolutely devoid of consciousness, and with no more feeling than the force which lifts the tides.

Next, in human affairs, in the relations of man

with man, in the conduct of life, in the events that occur, in human affairs generally everything happens by chance. No prudence in conduct, no wisdom or foresight can effect anything, for the most trivial circumstance will upset the deepest plan of the wisest mind. As Xenophon observed in old times, wisdom is like casting dice and determining your course by the number that appears. Virtue, humanity, the best and most beautiful conduct is wholly in vain. The history of thousands of years demonstrates it. In all these years there is no more moving instance on record than that of Danae, when she was dragged to the precipice, two thousand years ago. Sophron was governor of Ephesus, and Laodice plotted to assassinate him. Danae discovered the plot, and warned Sophron, who fled, and saved his life. Laodice—the murderess in intent—had Danae seized and cast from a cliff. On the verge Danae said that some persons despised the deity, and they might now prove the justice of their contempt by her fate. For having saved the man who was to her as a husband, she was rewarded in this way with cruel death by the deity, but Laodice was advanced to honour. The bitterness of these words remains to this hour.

In truth the deity, if responsible for such a thing, or for similar things, which occur now, should be despised. One must always despise the fatuous belief in such a deity. But as everything in human affairs obviously happens by chance, it is clear that no deity is responsible. If the deity guides chance in that manner, then let the deity be despised. Apparently the deity does not interfere, and all things happen by chance. I cease, therefore, to look for traces of the deity in life, because no such traces exist.

I conclude that there is an existence, a something higher than soul—higher, better, and more perfect than deity. Earnestly I pray to find this something better than a god. There is something superior, higher, more good. For this I search, labour, think, and pray. If after all there be nothing, and my soul has to go out like a flame, yet even then I have thought this while it lives. With the whole force of my existence, with the whole force of my thought, mind, and soul, I pray to find this Highest Soul, this greater than deity, this better than god. Give me to live the deepest soul-life now and always with this Soul. For want of words I write soul, but I think that it is something beyond soul.

POWER

Tuesday, the eagle I'd just hit with my car punctured my wrist with its talon. Today is Friday. The swelling has gone down and I can type again. I didn't see the eagle feeding on a road-killed deer north of Cokeville, Wyoming, because I took my eyes off the road for a few seconds to look down at my odometer. A large dark figure flashed from below on my right. The cracking I heard as I hit the eagle—I knew it was an eagle because there is nothing that flies that is that big and dark—was my grill shattering on impact. In my mirror, I watched the eagle spin in slow motion before landing in the breakdown lane. Feeling like shit, I stopped, turned around, and drove back, needing at least to pay my respects to the eagle and move it off the road. I parked ten feet away. The eagle had landed perfectly, as if placed by a mortician for viewing—on its back, wings folded softly at its sides, talons parallel and upright. Moving closer I saw that the eagle was breathing—gasping actually, its beak flexing open and closed with each breath, a gurgling sound coming from deep in its chest. I held its head as blood slowly dripped from its mouth, forming a small puddle on the asphalt. I didn't know what to do. I'd hit the eagle with such force that my grill lay scattered in a dozen pieces. How could the eagle have survived? I thought about ending its misery, but didn't know how. It stared up at me with its right eye. I put my other hand on its chest and felt each troubled breath. I'll stay here until it dies, I thought. Very few cars drove by, but one of them stopped and turned around. "Are you all right?" an older local couple asked.

"No," I said. "I hit this bird."

"What is it?" the man asked.

"A golden eagle," I said. "I think it will die soon."

"We're sorry," they said, and drove off.

Either the eagle was close to dying or it was getting better, because it seemed to breathe easier. I went back to my car to get a piece of cardboard. My plan was to gently tilt the bird, slide the cardboard under it, and slide it off of the road. Cars and trucks speeding by stressed the eagle and it struggled to lift its head.

I tried calming it by stroking its head and chest while it stared up at me with what seemed to be a "who the hell are you" look in its eyes. I carefully lifted its left side and was able to position the cardboard under its body.

The moment I started pulling the cardboard toward the roadside, the eagle erupted feet first, sinking one sharp talon deep into my wrist. I panicked, a huge angry bird stuck to me, and tried to quickly figure out the angle I needed to separate myself from the hook-like claw.

We struggled, the bird and I, and then suddenly I was free. The eagle landed in a heap, closer to traffic than before, breathing heavily again, calm—no panic in its eyes meeting mine with a burning, laser-like glare which said, "don't fuck with me again."

A man in a pickup with Idaho plates stopped and got out. "Can you believe how beautiful?" I said.

"Yep," he said, moving back to his truck. He got some heavy gloves and, without hesitating, firmly grasped both sides of the bird's body, picked the eagle up, and placed it gently on the snow out of harm's way. The eagle didn't have much struggle left. "They might be able to rehabilitate it," the man from Idaho said. "But I doubt it." I thanked him and he left.

I stayed with the eagle for half an hour more, hoping a highway patrol officer would come by. There was no cell service. The eagle didn't move much. Finally, I gave up and drove to the truck stop in Cokeville. When I asked them to call Game and Fish, they said that the older couple already had.

I remembered from first aid that puncture wounds should be allowed to bleed to forestall infection. I massaged the hole in my arm for a few minutes but managed only a few good drops. Although that talon had the sharpness of a hypodermic needle, it certainly wasn't as sterile. Plus, the talon seemed to have hit a muscle or tendon, and the area around my wound was swelling and bruised.

I called Terry but got voicemail. I left her the short version of the events. By the time she called back, she'd already researched the symbolic meaning of the dying eagle, the oozing hole in my arm. *"Eagle energy is about seeing things from a new perspective, a higher perspective,"* she read to me, "*and reclaiming personal power, a state of being reached through inner work. Broaden your sense of self.*" I realized that the shock and sadness and anger I carried from hitting that beautiful eagle trumped any deeper meaning and archetypal consequence. "I looked up the 'contrary eagle'—you did kill it, after all," she said. She explained that while normally these totems are positive, about our strengths, our weaknesses—shadows—may be equally important. "The contrary eagle medicine means that *You have forgotten your power and connectedness…you have failed to recognize that light is always available to those seeking illumination. Fasting and praying and vision quest may be necessary. You need to make more use of your inner abilities.* Brooke," she said, "this may be one of the most important things that has ever happened to you.

"Be sure," she added, "to take care of your *stigmata.*"

Last September, Terry and I had alternated reading Chapter V to each other, naked, sharing the afternoon sun with flat rocks during low tide in Downeast Maine. I triggered last fall when Terry read the part where Jefferies separates humans from all other life: "anti" or "ultra" or "outré-human," are terms he uses. I couldn't believe that he and I could disagree on something so basic and important.

I must be past the shock I'd had on hearing it for the first time. That, or the eagle injected new understanding through the hole it made in my arm. The couple who stopped to make sure I was okay probably didn't see beyond the eagle gasping for its last breath—nor my need to remember my personal power. And I'm sure the mythological, archetypal, or symbolic dimensions of that eagle never crossed the mind of that young man from Idaho.

What would Jefferies think? He seems to fall into the abyss of believing that humans are special on earth, which is not so different from what most people—especially modern Americans—believe today. Were he living today, would he make statements like:

I am separate all together from these designless things. The soul cannot be wrested down to them.

The next morning back in the desert, I wander outside. I notice the broken grill on my car. There is no doubt that I hit the eagle. There are those coming from our modern, exceptional system of belief who would say that all I did was hit the eagle and that the world now has one less eagle. A different belief suggests that not only is this bird a magnificent feathered creature with wings that span seven feet and eyes that can see a rabbit in a bush from a mile in the sky, an eagle is archetypal, embodies symbol and spirit, carries messages to the gods, and has entered our dreams for 200,000 years. The former belief system now threatens our collective lives. The latter can save us. The latter belief system gives access to information that, used properly, might allow us and those coming after us to thrive. The former says we are contained within and limited to existing knowledge and understanding, because we can know everything; the latter, that we don't and can't know everything, but that we come from stardust and are part of the cosmos.

What if Terry and I are wrong in believing that worlds exist beyond this obvious one, that our unconscious life is rich and detailed and larger by dimensions than our conscious life? What if the eagle was just another eagle? I don't care. Believing in mystery is believing in possibility.

In this chapter, Jefferies revisits *soul, immortality*, and *diety*, the three steppingstones of the caveman introduced earlier. He's searching for a fourth idea—something beyond the caveman.

We haven't moved beyond these ideas, Jefferies writes, for twelve thousand years because these ideas have been encumbered with superstition.

That "twelve thousand years" may be Jefferies referring to that important time when our hunting and gathering ancestors settled down to agriculture, resulting in what we now call civilization. Jung's idea that the collective unconscious contains the entire evolutionary history of our species came after Jefferies. What would Jung say about the three steppingstones of the caveman? In the introduction to his 1948 book, *The Nature Diaries and Notebooks of Richard Jefferies*, Samuel Looker suggests that "the general tenor of Jefferies' cogitations on these matters (soul, psyche, spirit, etc.) is very much in line with the reasoning of the greatest of all modern psychologists,

C.G. Jung," and when considered in that context, "are truly remarkable."

In 1909, Jung had a dream in which he discovered a cave in the basement of a house. There were bones in the cave, and two skulls, and Neolithic tools. Unlike Jefferies, who seems convinced that our problems may stem from our inability to move beyond the ideas of the caveman, Jung bases many of his ideas—about the collective unconscious, the psyche, our ability to save ourselves—on his theory that the caveman lives inside each of us. Jung calls the caveman the "Two Million Year-old Man." Jefferies suggests the need to move beyond the caveman, whereas Jung believes our deepest problems are rooted in our having cut ourselves off from this caveman dwelling within us. "Encumbrances" and "superstitions" to Jefferies were "archetypes" and "myths" to Jung, who contends that dreams provide us with access to that prehistoric, instinctive past—the collective unconscious—where the only tools we need for survival are kept.

Jefferies sees himself at the mouth of that cave, face to face with nature and himself. He acknowledges his soul's immortal existence and the importance of a fourth idea, even if he doesn't know what it is. He realizes "a soul-life illimitable."

"Soul-life" is a term that Jefferies uses frequently throughout, and is, according to scholars, the leading thought of *The Story of My Heart*. According to H.S. Salt in his 1905 biography *Richard Jefferies: His Life*

& his Ideals, soul-life is above and beyond the ideas of existence and immortality, beyond even deity itself; a spiritual entity which is even now realized in part by the absorption of the soul, in rapturous moments of reverie and devotion, into the beauty and infinity of the visible universe.

I can *feel* what soul-life is, but I would have a tough time explaining it. In *The Story of My Heart*, Jefferies often refers to elements of his "inner consciousness"—his unconscious—which suggests that he's made them conscious. According to Jung, the goal of every living person is to bring as much unconscious material as possible up to the light of day. He called this the process of *individuation*. This includes going into the "cave" for the archaic elements, the contents of the "collective unconscious" upon which our survival depends. I wonder if Jung might equate Jefferies' soul-life with his own idea of individuation.

We now have the knowledge that, due to climate change, our species faces an uncertain and challenging future. We know that due to our numbers, our technologies, and our greed, we have brought this on ourselves. We know that biological evolution is too slow to depend on for the adaptations required to save us. Civilization requires that we look outside for answers to these problems. Jung and Jefferies, with their theories on individuation and soul-life, respectively, beckon us to look *inside*.

"A great life," Jefferies wrote, "for an entire civilization, lies just outside the pale of common thought."

My attraction to Jefferies is based on his descriptions of experiences he had which are similar to my own, but also because he forces me to consider my beliefs. I grew up with a man-like god who watches over us and helps us if and when we're worthy. I grew up on an earth created in seven thousand years, and with books of scripture I was required to read and, in some cases, memorize. As hard as I tried, I couldn't make my own early experience in the wilds, immersed in the fully functioning natural system as part of the life force, mesh with what I was being taught on Sunday. For as long as I have a memory, my study has been directed toward sources that help me put words to how I feel and what I inherently know.

What do I believe? I believe there is a force moving all life toward something that works, something good. Call it God or deity, or the Great Mystery. Call it whatever you want. I agree with Darwin when he said, "we're not smart enough to comprehend something as complicated as 'God.'" I believe that creating a god in our image is the worst possible wrong.

CHAPTER V

~

It is not possible to narrate these incidents of the mind in strict order. I must now return to a period earlier than anything already narrated, and pass in review other phases of my search from then up till recently. So long since that I have forgotten the date, I used every morning to visit a spot where I could get a clear view of the east. Immediately on rising I went out to some elms; thence I could see across the dewy fields to the distant hill over or near which the sun rose. These elms partially hid me, for at that time I had a dislike to being seen, feeling that I should be despised if I was noticed. This happened once or twice, and I knew I was watched contemptuously, though no one had the least idea of my object. But I went every morning, and was satisfied if I could get two or three minutes to think unchecked. Often I saw the sun rise over the line of the hills, but if it was summer the sun had been up a long time.

I looked at the hills, at the dewy grass, and then up through the elm branches to the sky. In a moment all that was behind me, the house, the people, the sounds, seemed to disappear, and to leave me alone. Involuntarily I drew a long breath, then I breathed slowly. My thought, or inner consciousness, went up through the

illumined sky, and I was lost in a moment of exaltation. This only lasted a very short time, perhaps only
part of a second, and while it lasted there was no formulated wish. I was absorbed; I drank the beauty of
the morning; I was exalted. When it ceased I did wish
for some increase or enlargement of my existence to
correspond with the largeness of feeling I had momentarily enjoyed. Sometimes the wind came through
the tops of the elms, and the slender boughs bent, and
gazing up through them, and beyond the fleecy clouds,
I felt lifted up. The light coming across the grass and
leaving itself on the dew-drops, the sound of the wind,
and the sense of mounting to the lofty heaven, filled
me with a deep sigh, a wish to draw something out of
the beauty of it, some part of that which caused my
admiration, the subtle inner essence.

Sometimes the green tips of the highest boughs
seemed gilded, the light laid a gold on the green. Or
the trees bowed to a stormy wind roaring through
them, the grass threw itself down, and in the east
broad curtains of a rosy tint stretched along. The light
was turned to redness in the vapour, and rain hid the
summit of the hill. In the rush and roar of the stormy
wind the same exaltation, the same desire, lifted me
for a moment. I went there every morning, I could not
exactly define why; it was like going to a rose bush to
taste the scent of the flower and feel the dew from its
petals on the lips. But I desired the beauty—the inner
subtle meaning—to be in me, that I might have it, and

with it an existence of a higher kind.

Later on I began to have daily pilgrimages to think these things. There was a feeling that I must go somewhere, and be alone. It was a necessity to have a few minutes of this separate life every day; my mind required to live its own life apart from other things. A great oak at a short distance was one resort, and sitting on the grass at the roots, or leaning against the trunk and looking over the quiet meadows towards the bright southern sky, I could live my own life a little while. Behind the trunk I was alone; I liked to lean against it; to touch the lichen on the rough bark. High in the wood of branches the birds were not alarmed; they sang, or called, and passed to and fro happily. The wind moved the leaves, and they replied to it softly; and now at this distance of time I can see the fragments of sky up through the boughs. Bees were always humming in the green field; ring-doves went over swiftly, flying for the woods.

Of the sun I was conscious; I could not look at it, but the boughs held back the beams so that I could feel the sun's presence pleasantly. They shaded the sun, yet let me know that it was there. There came to me a delicate, but at the same time a deep, strong, and sensuous enjoyment of the beautiful green earth, the beautiful sky and sun; I felt them, they gave me inexpressible delight, as if they embraced and poured out their love upon me. It was I who loved them, for my heart was broader than the earth; it is broader now than even then, more thirsty and desirous. After the sensuous enjoyment always came the thought, the desire: That I might be like this; that I might have the inner meaning of the sun, the light, the earth, the trees and grass, translated into some growth of excellence in myself, both of body and of mind; greater perfection of physique, greater perfection of mind and soul; that I might be higher in myself. To this oak I came daily for a long time; sometimes only for a minute, for just to view the spot was enough. In the bitter cold of spring, when the north wind blackened everything, I used to come now and then at night to look from under the bare branches at the splendour of the southern sky. The stars burned with brilliance, broad Orion and flashing Sirius—there are more or brighter constellations visible then than all the year: and the clearness of the air and the blackness of the sky—black, not clouded—let them gleam in their fullness. They lifted me—they gave me fresh vigour of soul. Not all that the stars could have given, had they been destinies, could have satiated me. This, all this, and more, I wanted in myself.

There was a place a mile or so along the road where the hills could be seen much better; I went there frequently to think the same thought. Another spot was by an elm, a very short walk, where openings in the trees, and the slope of the ground, brought the hills well into view. This too, was a favourite thinking-place. Another was a wood, half an hour's walk distant, through part of which a rude track went, so that it was not altogether inclosed. The ash-saplings, and the trees, the firs, the hazel bushes—to be among these enabled me to be myself. From the buds of spring to the berries of autumn, I always liked to be there. Sometimes in spring there was a sheen of blue-bells covering acres; the doves cooed; the blackbirds whistled sweetly; there was a taste of green things in the air. But it was the tall firs that pleased me most; the glance rose up the flame-shaped fir-tree, tapering to its green tip, and above was the azure sky. By aid of the tree I felt the sky more. By aid of everything beautiful I felt myself, and in that intense sense of consciousness prayed for greater perfection of soul and body.

Afterwards, I walked almost daily more than two miles along the road to a spot where the hills began, where from the first rise the road could be seen winding southwards over the hills, open and uninclosed. I paused a minute or two by a clump of firs, in whose branches the wind always sighed—there is always a movement of the air on a hill. Southwards the sky was illumined by the sun, southwards the clouds moved across the opening or pass in the amphitheatre, and southwards, though far distant, was the sea. There I could think a moment. These pilgrimages gave me a few sacred minutes daily; the moment seemed holy when the thought or desire came in its full force.

A time came when, having to live in a town, these pilgrimages had to be suspended. The wearisome work on which I was engaged would not permit of them. But I used to look now and then, from a window, in the evening at a birch-tree at some distance; its graceful boughs drooped across the glow of the sunset. The thought was not suspended; it lived in me always. A bitterer time still came when it was necessary to be separated from those I loved. There is little indeed in the more immediate suburbs of London to gratify the sense of the beautiful. Yet there was a cedar by which I used to walk up and down, and think the same thoughts as under the great oak in the solitude of the sunlit meadows. In the course of slow time happier circumstances brought us together again, and, though near London, at a spot where there was easy access to meadows and woods. Hills that purify those who walk on them there were not. Still I thought my old thoughts.

I was much in London, and, engagements completed, I wandered about in the same way as in the woods of former days. From the stone bridges I looked down on the river; the gritty dust, the straws that lie on the bridges, flew up and whirled round with every gust from the flowing tide; gritty dust that settles in the nostrils and on the lips, the very residuum of all that is repulsive in the greatest city of the world. The noise of the traffic and the constant pressure from the crowds passing, their incessant and disjointed talk, could not distract me. One moment at least I had, a moment when I thought of the push of the great sea forcing the water to flow under the feet of these crowds, the distant sea strong and splendid; when I saw the sunlight gleam on the tidal wavelets; when I felt the wind, and was conscious of the earth, the sea, the sun, the air, the immense forces working on, while the city hummed by the river. Nature was deepened by the crowds and foot-worn stones. If the tide had ebbed, and the masts of the vessels were tilted as the hulls rested on the shelving mud, still even the blackened mud did not prevent me seeing the water as water flowing to the sea. The sea had drawn down, and the wavelets washing the strand here as they hastened were running the faster to it. Eastwards from London Bridge the river raced to the ocean.

The bright morning sun of summer heated the eastern parapet of London Bridge; I stayed in the recess to acknowledge it. The smooth water was a broad sheen of light, the built-up river flowed calm and silent by a thousand doors, rippling only where the stream chafed against a chain. Red pennants drooped, gilded vanes gleamed on polished masts, black-pitched hulls glistened like a black rook's feathers in sunlight; the clear air cut out the forward angles of the warehouses, the shadowed wharves were quiet in shadows that carried light; far down the ships that were hauling out moved in repose, and with the stream floated away into the summer mist. There was a faint blue colour in the air hovering between the built-up banks, against the lit walls, in the hollows of the houses. The swallows wheeled and climbed, twittered and glided downwards. Burning on, the great sun stood in the sky, heating the parapet, glowing steadfastly upon me as when I rested in the narrow valley grooved out in prehistoric times. Burning on steadfast, and ever present as my thought. Lighting the broad river, the broad walls; lighting the least speck of dust; lighting the great heaven; gleaming on my fingernail. The fixed point of day—the sun. I was intensely conscious of it; I felt it; I felt the presence of the immense powers of the universe; I felt out into the depths of the ether. So intensely conscious of the sun, the sky, the limitless space, I felt too in the midst of eternity then, in the midst of the supernatural, among the immortal, and the greatness of the material realised the spirit. By these I saw my soul; by these I knew the supernatural to be more intensely real than the sun. I touched the supernatural, the immortal, there that moment.

When, weary of walking on the pavements, I went to rest in the National Gallery, I sat and rested before one or other of the human pictures. I am not a picture lover: they are flat surfaces, but those that I call human are nevertheless beautiful. The knee in *Daphnis and Chloe* and the breast are like living things; they draw the heart towards them, the heart must love them. I lived in looking; without beauty there is no life for me, the divine beauty of flesh is life itself to me. The shoulder in the Surprise, the rounded rise of the bust, the exquisite tints of the ripe skin, momentarily gratified the sea-thirst in me. For I thirst with all the thirst of the salt sea, and the sun-heated sands dry for the tide, with all the sea I thirst for beauty. And I know full well that one lifetime, however long, cannot fill my heart. My throat and tongue and whole body have often been parched and feverish dry with this measureless thirst, and again moist to the fingers' ends like a sappy bough. It burns in me as the sun burns in the sky.

The glowing face of Cytherea in Titian's *Venus and Adonis*, the heated cheek, the lips that kiss each eye that gazes on them, the desiring glance, the golden hair—sunbeams moulded into features—this face answered me. Juno's wide back and mesial groove, is any thing so lovely as the back? Cytherea's poised hips unveiled for judgment; these called up the same thirst I felt on the green sward in the sun, on the wild beach listening to the quiet sob as the summer wave drank at the land. I will search the world through for beauty. I came here and sat to rest before these in the days when I could not afford to buy so much as a glass of ale, weary and faint from walking on stone pavements. I came later on, in better times, often straight from labours which though necessary will ever be distasteful, always to rest my heart with loveliness. I go still; the divine beauty of flesh is life itself to me. It was, and is, one of my London pilgrimages.

Another was to the Greek sculpture galleries in the British Museum. The statues are not, it is said, the best; broken too, and mutilated, and seen in a dull, commonplace light. But they were shape—divine shape of man and woman; the form of limb and torso, of bust and neck, gave me a sighing sense of rest. These were they who would have stayed with me under the shadow of the oaks while the blackbirds fluted and the south air swung the cowslips. They would have walked with me among the reddened gold of the wheat. They would have rested with me on the hilltops and in the narrow valley grooved of ancient times. They would have listened with me to the sob of the summer sea drinking the land. These had thirsted of sun, and earth, and sea, and sky. Their shape spoke this thirst and desire like mine—if I had lived with them from Greece till now I should not have had enough of them. Tracing the form of limb and torso with the eye gave me a sense of rest.

Sometimes I came in from the crowded streets and ceaseless hum; one glance at these shapes and I became myself. Sometimes I came from the Reading-room, where under the dome I often looked up from the desk and realised the crushing hopelessness of books, useless, not equal to one bubble borne along on the running brook I had walked by, giving no thought like the spring when I lifted the water in my hand and saw the light gleam on it. Torso and limb, bust and neck instantly returned me to myself; I felt as I did lying on the turf listening to the wind among the grass; it would have seemed natural to have found butterflies fluttering among he statues. The same deep desire was with me. I shall always go to speak to them; they are a place of pilgrimage; wherever there is a beautiful statue there is a place of pilgrimage.

I always stepped aside, too, to look awhile at the head of Julius Caesar. The domes of the swelling temples of his broad head are full of mind, evident to the eye as a globe is full of substance to the sense of feeling in the hands that hold it. The thin worn cheek is entirely human; endless difficulties surmounted by endless labour are marked in it, as the sandblast, by dint of particles ceaselessly driven, carves the hardest material. If circumstances favoured him he made those circumstances his own by marvellous labour, so as justly to receive the credit of chance. Therefore the thin cheek is entirely human—the sum of human life made visible in one face—labour, and endurance, and mind, and all in vain. A shadow—of deep sadness has gathered on it in the years that have passed, because endurance was without avail. It is sadder to look at than the grass-grown tumulus I used to sit by, because it is a personality, and also on account of the extreme folly of our human race ever destroying our greatest.

Far better had they endeavoured, however hopelessly, to keep him living till this day. Did but the race this hour possess one-hundredth part of his breadth of view, how happy for them! Of whom else can it be said that he had no enemies to forgive because he recognised no enemy? Nineteen hundred years ago he put in actual practice, with more arbitrary power than any despot, those very principles of humanity which are now put forward as the highest culture. But he made them to be actual things under his sway.

The one man filled with mind; the one man without avarice, anger, pettiness, littleness; the one man generous and truly great of all history. It is enough to make one despair to think of the mere brutes butting to death the great-minded Caesar. He comes nearest to the ideal of a design-power arranging the affairs of the world for good in practical things. Before his face—the divine brow of mind above, the human suffering-drawn cheek beneath—my own thought became set and strengthened. That I could but look at things in the broad way he did; that I could not possess one particle of such width of intellect to guide my own course, to cope with and drag forth from the iron-resisting forces of the universe some one thing of my prayer for the soul and for the flesh.

PILGRIM

Terry and I scheduled two weeks apart in January to write—I'm in southern Utah, while she's home in Wyoming. We learned early the importance of physical space in our marriage—how creativity blossoms when we're alone, each on our own natural schedule. The timing was perfect—Terry and I needing solitude and the dogs needing a break from the vise winter had put on Jackson Hole.

Consecutive sunny days opened paths in the snow while creating serious mud. If I get out early with the dogs and plan carefully, we can walk for an hour before the ground thaws. This morning, after a quick read of Chapter V, we're out the back door into blazing sun. We hurry between sage and rabbit brush and up the dike, built to hold back floodwaters when this valley was a massive ranch. We slide on snow down into the gash where some skillful backhoe work by a neighbor channels current floods, and climb up the other side. Finding our way between Russian thistle, the latest "plague" (grasshoppers one year, an exotic mustard plant that choked off all of our trails the next, and the worst of all: cutworm caterpillars which covered every surface for weeks) and over the barbed wire fence separating private land from public, where cows graze. During the long, quiet stretch, the word "pilgrimage" blossoms in my head. It's been stuck there since reading Chapter V in *The Story of My Heart*.

"Pilgrimage," for me, was an old, religious term until I came across the phrase "the plane of meaning."[1] If a dozen people are having the same outward experience, their own inner experiences may be spread out along a "plane," in relation to their own "center." A commercial river trip is a good example: Take five random people on a raft. One of them may be a *recreational* tourist, seeking only entertainment, for the same reason she goes to a movie or a game: recreation allows her to return refreshed to the wear and tear of her center.

Next to her, a young man is having a *diversional* experience. He isn't looking for meaning, but wants to escape the boredom and routine of his life.

One woman wonders if being a river guide would be a better life than the one she currently has writing computer code for a pharmaceutical company. Consider her an *experiential* tourist.

The *experimental* tourist no longer acknowledges being part of her society but is actively engaged in a search for an alternative for her center.

The *existential* tourist, or pilgrim, is fully committed to an alternative spiritual center external to that of her culture and society. For pilgrims, traveling is a spiritual practice to access places of higher meaning.

---

1. Norman, Alex (2011-09-22). *Spiritual Tourism: Travel and Religious Practice in Western Society* (Continuum Advances in Religious Studies) (p. 43). Continuum UK. Kindle Edition.

Pilgrims are dedicated to the wellbeing of others and the planet.

According to this definition, Jefferies is a pilgrim, although the term "existential tourist" is so academic that it seems offensive when applied to him.

In Chapter V, Jefferies describes his pilgrimages as the familiar landscapes where he discovers higher meaning. These include a high spot from which he gets a clear view, a great oak he sits against, a wood a half-mile from his home where he could be alone, a road winding south through the hills along which he always paused to feel wind sighing through tree branches.

Every walk Jefferies took couldn't have been a pilgrimage. God knows that Jefferies had plenty to think about, suffering as he did throughout his life from what he described as the "Three Giants" against him—"disease, despair, and poverty." And while *The Story of My Heart* is inspired—seems to have leapt from his inner consciousness toward the end of his life—most of the five hundred articles/essays, and thirty books he wrote to feed his family had to do with farming and worker politics, requiring serious research and analysis.

Jefferies' plane of meaning might have had four positions.

Some days, he needed a *refuge* from what his family and neighbors expected of him. Toward the end of his life, when illness challenged him physically, *suffering* had to have greatly influenced his experience. He thinks about farm prospects and labor from a *practi-*

cal point of view. At another level, he's inspired. He's on his pilgrimage—having *existential* experiences. He writes, "My thought, or inner consciousness went up through the illumined sky, and I was lost in a moment of exaltation." So, "thought" to Jefferies is also his inner consciousness, his unconscious emerging.

Reading about the walks Jefferies took reminds me of the ten or twelve familiar routes around our house where I walk regularly, either alone or with Terry—always with our dogs—that inspire me.

When I was younger, with less-meaningful work, I needed adventure to stay sane. Weekend powder skiing, canyoneering, running in the Salt Lake foothills were both diversional and recreational—I was able to forget about the plumbing supplies I sold all week and have fun with solid friends.

My experiences became exploratory when we found new places permeated by a strong sense of the unknown, expanding our concept of what was possible; then extreme and more dangerous when I needed to ski deeper and steeper, and wander further into vast desert creases in order to feel alive.

My experiential experience was with my own body: what was it capable of doing? How far and fast could I push it? How would it respond? How quickly would it recover?

My passion for risk and physical strength evolved toward addiction. I chuckled each morning as I prepared to go skiing when Terry would call the Avalanche forecast number and relay what she heard on the recording about the day's conditions. "Brooke," she'd say, "there's significant temperature gradients, leading to unstable conditions on northern exposures above eight thousand feet. You'll stay away from northern exposures, won't you?" She said she always planned my funeral while I was away skiing, only to be happily surprised when I safely returned. We knew of too many who didn't return safely and read too many obituaries of people who "died doing what they loved." I'm not sure exactly what motivated me, but one day I realized that dying doing what I loved and leaving Terry sad and alone was not acceptable and vowed to eliminate what physical risk I could control.

Rio, our Basenji, came into our lives and helped me to shift radically away from my extreme, physical treks, possibly saving my life. He didn't like snow and when we hiked in the desert he'd run off when canyon walls got too high or too narrow. We discovered a different kind of adventure involving real seeing— noticing the changes along familiar trails. Walking with friends became a communal experience, where we softened enough to discuss ideas in new ways and deal with uncomfortable issues creatively. Ironically, my plane of meaning expanded closer to home.

Some days, out with our dogs—Rio, and now Winslow Homer, a Chihuahua mix we rescued over a year ago—my experience touches on the existential. Familiar ground and routine frees up space in my head.

Instead of focusing narrowly on where I'm going, what I'm doing, am I safe, my mind opens up like a net, trapping vaporous ideas and concepts. If I'm lucky, these might crystallize into useful, fruitful inspiration. What has been unconscious becomes conscious. That's if I'm careful not to let my dwindling bank account, the broken car, or leaking roof hijack my thoughts.

Being out with Terry is always existential. This can be frustrating. I think that she's constantly on pilgrimage. Goals or destinations don't matter, as we rarely reach them together. We'll be walking along and suddenly she'll stop to write some thought in her journal, or watch a bird. I've watched her follow a lizard for an hour. Sometimes I'll sit quietly with her. Other times, I'll need to move, and I leave her alone. Once, we were hiking in northern Spain, in an area known for the raptors living there. We'd hiked less than a mile when we saw, high in the sky, dozens of huge griffon vultures soaring in a large group. We lay down on the ground and watched them through our binoculars. "Let's go," I said. "Go ahead," she said. "I'm happy here." I went off on my own and an hour later came over a rise and looked out toward Terry. What I saw frightened me. The vultures that had been soaring high overhead had dropped to what seemed like a few feet above Terry, who had fallen asleep. "Terry," I yelled, frantic. "Wake up! They think you're dead!" Later, she told me what an amazing dream I'd interrupted.

Ezra Pound says the "natural object is always the

adequate symbol." He was referring to poetry, but couldn't this apply to everything we're exposed to while on pilgrimage, during our wild moments coming alive in our solitude? Immersed in the thousands of different, constant processes making up any natural system, the particular elements—objects—attracting our attention may be our unconscious bubbling to the surface inspiring us onward.

Jefferies writes:

> The light coming across the grass and leaving itself on the dew-drops, the sound of the wind, and the sense of mounting to the lofty heaven, filled me with a deep sigh, a wish to draw something out of the beauty of it, some part of that which caused my admiration, the subtle inner essence.

We are in agreement.

CHAPTER VI

~

There is a place in front of the Royal Exchange where the wide pavement reaches out like a promontory. It is in the shape of a triangle with a rounded apex. A stream of traffic runs on either side, and other streets send their currents down into the open space before it. Like the spokes of a wheel converging streams of human life flow into this agitated pool. Horses and carriages, carts, vans, omnibuses, cabs, every kind of conveyance cross each other's course in every possible direction. Twisting in and out by the wheels and under the horses' heads, working a devious way, men and women of all conditions wind a path over. They fill the interstices between the carriages and blacken the surface, till the vans almost float on human beings. Now the streams slacken, and now they rush amain, but never cease; dark waves are always rolling down the incline opposite, waves swell out from the side rivers, all London converges into this focus. There is an indistinguishable noise—it is not clatter, hum, or roar, it is not resolvable; made up of a thousand thousand footsteps, from a thousand hoofs, a thousand wheels—of haste, and shuffle, and quick movements, and ponderous loads; no attention can resolve it into a fixed sound.

Blue carts and yellow omnibuses, varnished carriages and brown vans, green omnibuses and red cabs, pale loads of yellow straw, rusty-red iron clanking on paintless carts, high white wool-packs, grey horses, bay horses, black teams; sunlight sparkling on brass harness, gleaming from carriage panels; jingle, jingle, jingle! An intermixed and intertangled, ceaselessly changing jingle, too, of colour; flecks of colour champed, as it were, like bits in the horses' teeth, frothed and strewn about, and a surface always of dark-dressed people winding like the curves on fast-flowing water. This is the vortex and whirlpool, the centre of human life today on the earth. Now the tide rises and now it sinks, but the flow of these rivers always continues. Here it seethes and whirls, not for an hour only, but for all present time, hour by hour, day by day, year by year.

Here it rushes and pushes, the atoms triturate and grind, and, eagerly thrusting by, pursue their separate ends. Here it appears in its unconcealed personality, indifferent to all else but itself, absorbed and rapt in eager self, devoid and stripped of conventional gloss and politeness, yielding only to get its own way; driving, pushing, carried on in a stress of feverish force like a bullet, dynamic force apart from reason or will, like the force that lifts the tides and sends the clouds onwards. The friction of a thousand interests evolves a condition of electricity in which men are moved to and fro without considering their steps. Yet the agitated pool of life is stonily indifferent, the thought is absent or preoccupied, for it is evident that the mass are unconscious of the scene in which they act.

But it is more sternly real than the very stones, for all these men and women that pass through are driven on by the push of accumulated circumstances; they cannot stay, they must go, their necks are in the slave's ring, they are beaten like seaweed against the solid walls of fact. In ancient times, Xerxes, the king of kings, looking down upon his myriads, wept to think that in a hundred years not one of them would be left. Where will be these millions of today in a hundred years? But, further than that, let us ask, Where then will be the sum and outcome of their labour? If they wither away like summer grass, will not at least a result be left which those of a hundred years hence may be the better for? No, not one jot! There will not be any sum or outcome or result of this ceaseless labour and movement; it vanishes in the moment that it is done, and in a hundred years nothing will be there, for nothing is there now. There will be no more sum or result than accumulates from the motion of a revolving cowl on a housetop. Nor do they receive any more sunshine during their lives, for they are unconscious of the sun.

I used to come and stand near the apex of the promontory of pavement, which juts out towards the pool of life; I still go there to ponder. Burning in the sky, the sun shone on me as when I rested in the narrow valley carved in prehistoric time. Burning in the sky, I can never forget the sun. The heat of summer is dry there as if the light carried an impalpable dust; dry, breathless heat that will not let the skin respire, but swathes up the dry fire in the blood. But beyond the heat and light, I felt the presence of the sun as I felt it in the solitary valley, the presence of the resistless forces of the universe; the sun burned in the sky as I stood and pondered. Is there any theory, philosophy, or creed, is there any system or culture, any formulated method able to meet and satisfy each separate item of this agitated pool of human life? By which they may be guided, by which hope, by which look forward? Not a mere illusion of the craven heart—something real, as real as the solid walls of fact against which, like drifted sea-weed, they are dashed; something to give each separate personality sunshine and a flower in its own existence now; something to shape this million-handed labour to an end and outcome that will leave more sunshine and more flowers to those who must succeed? Something real now, and not in the spirit-land; in this hour now, as I stand and the sun burns. Can any creed, philosophy, system, or culture endure the test and remain unmolten in this fierce focus of human life?

Consider, is there anything slowly painted on the once mystic and now commonplace papyri of ancient, ancient Egypt, held on the mummy's withered breast? In that elaborate ritual, in the procession of the symbols, in the winged circle, in the laborious sarcophagus? Nothing; absolutely nothing! Before the fierce heat of the human furnace, the papyri smoulder away as paper smoulders under a lens in the sun. Remember Nineveh and the cult of the fir-cone, the turbaned and bearded bulls of stone, the lion hunt, the painted chambers loaded with tile books, the lore of the arrow-headed writing. What is in Assyria? There are sand, and failing rivers, and in Assyria's writings an utter nothing. The aged caves of India, who shall tell when they were sculptured? Far back when the sun was burning, burning in the sky as now in untold precedent time. Is there any meaning in those ancient caves? The indistinguishable noise not to be resolved, born of the human struggle, mocks in answer.

In the strange characters of the Zend, in the San-scrit, in the effortless creed of Confucius, in the Aztec coloured-string writings and rayed stones, in the uncertain marks left of the sunken Polynesian continent, hieroglyphs as useless as those of Memphis, nothing. Nothing! They have been tried, and were found an illusion. Think then, today, now looking from this apex of the pavement promontory outwards from our own land to the utmost bounds of the farthest sail, is there any faith or culture at this hour, which can stand, in this fierce heat? From the various forms of Semitic, Aryan, or Turanian creed now existing, from the printing-press to the palm-leaf volume on to those who call on the jewel in the lotus, can aught be gathered which can face this, the Reality? The indistinguishable noise, non-resolvable, roars a loud contempt.

Turn, then, to the calm reasoning of Aristotle; is there anything in that? Can the half-divine thought of Plato, rising in storeys of sequential ideas, following each other to the conclusion, endure here? No! All the philosophers in Diogenes Laertius fade away: the theories of mediaeval days; the organon of experiment; down to this hour—they are useless alike. The science of this hour, drawn from the printing press in an endless web of paper, is powerless here; the indistinguishable noise echoed from the smoke-shadowed walls despises the whole. A thousand footsteps, a thousand hoofs, a thousand wheels roll over and utterly contemn them in complete annihilation. Mere illusions of heart or mind, they are tested and thrust aside by the irresistible push of a million converging feet.

Burning in the sky, the sun shines as it shone on me in the solitary valley, as it burned on when the earliest cave of India was carved. Above the indistinguishable roar of the many feet I feel the presence of the sun, of the immense forces of the universe, and beyond these the sense of the eternal now, of the immortal. Full well aware that all has failed, yet, side by side with the sadness of that knowledge, there lives on in me an unquenchable belief, thought burning like the sun, that there is yet something to be found, something real, something to give each separate personality sunshine and flowers in its own existence now. Something to shape this million-handed labour to an end and outcome, leaving accumulated sunshine and flowers to those who shall succeed. It must be dragged forth by might of thought from the immense forces of the universe.

To prepare for such an effort, first the mind must be cleared of the conceit that, because we live today, we are wiser than the ages gone. The mind must acknowledge its ignorance; all the learning and lore of so many eras must be erased from it as an encumbrance. It is not from past or present knowledge, science or faith, that it is to be drawn. Erase these altogether as they are erased under the fierce heat of the focus before me. Begin wholly afresh. Go straight to the sun, the immense forces of the universe, to the Entity unknown; go higher than a god; deeper than prayer; and open a new day. That I might but have a fragment of Caesar's intellect to find a fragment of this desire!

From my home near London I made a pilgrimage almost daily to an aspen by a brook. It was a mile and a quarter along the road, far enough for me to walk off the concentration of mind necessary for work. The idea of the pilgrimage was to get away from the endless and nameless circumstances of everyday existence, which by degrees build a wall about the mind so that it travels in a constantly narrowing circle. This tether of the faculties tends to make them accept present knowledge, and present things, as all that can be attained to. This is all—there is nothing more—is the iterated preaching of house-life. Remain; be content; go round and round in one barren path, a little money, a little food and sleep, some ancient fables, old age and death. Of all the inventions of casuistry with man for ages has in various ways which manacled himself, and stayed his own advance, there is none equally potent with the supposition that nothing more is possible. Once well impress on the mind that it has already all, that advance is impossible because there is nothing further, and it is chained like a horse to an iron pin in the ground. It is the most deadly—the most fatal poison of the mind. No such casuistry has ever for a moment held me, but still, if permitted, the constant routine of house-life, the same work, the same thought in the work, the little circumstances regularly recurring, will dull the keenest edge of thought. By my daily pilgrimage, I escaped from it back to the sun.

In summer the leaves of the aspen rustled pleasantly, there was the tinkle of falling water over a hatch, thrushes sang and blackbirds whistled, greenfinches laughed in their talk to each other. The commonplace dusty road was commonplace no longer. In the dust was the mark of the chaffinches' little feet; the white light rendered even the dust brighter to look on. The air came from the south-west—there were distant hills in that direction—over fields of grass and corn. As I visited the spot from day to day the wheat grew from green to yellow, the wild roses flowered, the scarlet poppies appeared, and again the beeches reddened in autumn. In the march of time there fell away from my mind, as the leaves from the trees in autumn, the last traces and relics of superstitions and traditions acquired compulsorily in childhood. Always feebly adhering, they finally disappeared.

There fell away, too, personal bias and prejudices, enabling me to see clearer and with wider sympathies. The glamour of modern science and discoveries faded away, for I found them no more than the first potter's wheel. Erasure and reception proceeded together; the past accumulations of casuistry were erased, and my thought widened to receive the idea of something beyond all previous ideas. With disbelief, belief increased. The aspiration and hope, the prayer, was the same as that which I felt years before on the hills, only it now broadened.

Experience of life, instead of curtailing and checking my prayer, led me to reject experience altogether. As well might the horse believe that the road the bridle forces it to traverse every day encircles the earth as I believe in experience. All the experience of the greatest city in the world could not withhold me. I rejected it wholly. I stood bare-headed before the sun, in the presence of the earth and air, in the presence of the immense forces of the universe. I demand that which will make me more perfect now, this hour. London convinced me of my own thought. That thought has always been with me, and always grows wider.

One midsummer I went out of the road into the fields, and sat down on the grass between the yellowing wheat and the green hawthorn bushes. The sun

I took up a piece of clod and crumbled it in my fingers—it was a joy to touch it—I held my hand so that I could see the sunlight gleam on the slightly moist surface of the skin. The earth and sun were to me like my flesh and blood, and the air of the sea life.

With all the greater existence I drew from them I prayed for a bodily life equal to it, for a soul-life beyond my thought, for my inexpressible desire of more than I could shape even into idea. There was something higher than idea, invisible to thought as air to the eye; give me bodily life equal in fullness to the strength of earth, and sun, and sea; give me the soul-life of my desire. Once more I went down to the sea, touched it, and said farewell. So deep was the inhalation of this life that day, that it seemed to remain in me for years. This was a real pilgrimage.

Time passed away, with more labour, pleasure, and again at last, after much pain and wearinesss of mind, I came down again to the sea. The circumstances were changed—it was not a hurried glance—there were opportunities for longer thought. It mattered scarcely anything to me now whether I was alone, or whether houses and other people were near. Nothing could disturb my inner vision. By the sea, aware of the sun overhead, and the blue heaven, I feel that there is nothing between me and space. This is the verge of a gulf, and a tangent from my feet goes straight unchecked into the unknown. It is the edge of the abyss as much as if the earth were cut away in a sheer fall of eight thousand miles to the sky beneath, thence a hollow to the stars. Looking straight out is looking straight down; the eye-glance gradually departs from the sea-level, and, rising as that falls, enters the hollow of heaven. It is gazing along the face of a vast precipice into the hollow space which is nameless.

There mystery has been placed, but realising the vast hollow yonder makes me feel that the mystery is here. I, who am here on the verge, standing on the margin of the sky, am in the mystery itself. If I let my eye look back upon me from the extreme opposite of heaven, then this spot where I stand is in the centre of the hollow. Alone with the sea and sky, I presently feel all the depth and wonder of the unknown come back surging up around, and touching me as the foam runs to my feet. I am in it now, not tomorrow, this moment; I cannot escape from it. Though I may deceive myself with labour, yet still I am in it; in sleep too. There is no escape from this immensity.

Feeling this by the sea, under the sun, my life enlarges and quickens, striving to take to itself the largeness of the heaven. The frame cannot expand, but the soul is able to stand before it. No giant's body could be in proportion to the earth, but a little spirit is equal to the entire cosmos, to earth and ocean, sun and star-hollow. These are but a few acres to it. Were the cosmos twice as wide, the soul could run over it, and return to itself in a time so small, no measure exists to mete it. Therefore, I think the soul may sometimes find out an existence as superior as my mind is to the dead chalk cliff.

With the great sun burning over the foam-flaked sea, roofed with heaven—aware of myself, a consciousness forced on me by these things—I feel that thought must yet grow larger and correspond in magnitude of conception to these. But these cannot content me, these Titanic things of sea, and sun, and profundity; I feel that my thought is stronger than they are. I burn life like a torch. The hot light shot back from the sea scorches my cheek—my life is burning in me. The soul throbs like the sea for a larger life. No thought which I have ever had has satisfied my soul.

IDLENESS

"With disbelief, belief increased." Is Jefferies saying that the space we have to hold our belief is limited and static, a vessel perhaps?

I love gathering small stones I find while wandering around the desert. This habit got out of hand and now I'm limited to one jar. Once filled, Terry and I agreed, I would need to take some stones back outside before I could bring any new ones in. While I'd like to keep them all, the jar cannot expand.

Were the thoughts, theories, and ideas Jefferies describes throughout *The Story of My Heart* only possible once he made room for them by abandoning earlier beliefs?

Growing up in the glare of the Mormon temple, Terry and I didn't develop or discover our beliefs, we inherited them. At birth, we received a list of rules which, if followed, would guarantee a good, moral life, and a phenomenally productive afterlife.

Both of us were born into families who are very active in the Mormon faith. But we both had those we loved and respected to whom doubt was positive and held possibility. I had a revered uncle and aunt whose unanswered questions about faith kept them away from church. Mimi's husband Jack, Terry's grandfather, had never been baptized, and Mimi, during the course of her continual inquiry, "read" herself out of the Mormon Church.

One of two things happened: Either those beliefs were pushed out by a new, more powerful sense of how life works that blossomed in us over time in the wild world; or these traditional beliefs merged with our experiences, forming a platform for our spiritual evolution. Together, Terry and I stepped off of that well-worn path into the great unknown. I doubt we would have had the courage to do it alone.

Jefferies' early life and his religious history are elusive. As a boy, Richard devoured Shakespeare and developed a deep, personal understanding of the Bible.

Jefferies writes, "I was not more than eighteen when an inner and esoteric meaning began to come to me from all the visible universe, and identifiable aspirations filled me."

He began reading Greek and Roman literature along with Plato. His home life was tense due to family financial difficulties, his lack of interest in the family farm, and his general disregard for work. He began arguing religion with his father (an "irregular church goer") while passing through "a stage of aggressive negation" and "was full of interest in ideas and evidently of confidence too." In fact, a neighbor recalled that when Jefferies did go to church after he and Jessie Baden were engaged, he insisted on using only "the Devil's Door" —the door "through which the Devil fled … from the baptized."

Like Jefferies, Terry and I were raised in and

around organized religion. Orthodoxy lost its influence over us once we began to taste and experience and understand the wild world. In a new sense, we fell in love.

The daily pilgrimages Jefferies made throughout his life provided him with enough evidence and material to form his own religion.

Since Jefferies' death, religious scholars and experts have struggled to categorize his philosophy. In *Richard Jefferies and the Ecological Vision* (2006), Brian Morris explores the boxes into which they've tried to squeeze Jefferies' thoughts, philosophy, and writings. By most definitions, the experiences Jefferies had were mystical. He sought out and felt the sense of wonder in the natural world, and the awe-inspiring powers of nature. He was not seeking union with God nor was he looking for detachment from the world in order to experience the void (*sunyata*) or pure consciousness of Buddhism. Was he a pantheist, equating "god" with the forces of nature and the universe? Definitely a pagan, a worshipper of nature, he was not a polytheist, who worships many gods. His particular mysticism has been tied to Zen Buddhism, Platonism, to *prana*, the Indian concept of breath or life force, and even St. Teresa of Avila's mystic tradition, when in fact, it may be all his own. He writes:

> Rapt in the fullness of the moment, I prayed there with all that expansion of mind and frame; no words, no definition, inexpressible

desire of physical life, of soul-life, equal to and beyond the highest imagining of my heart.

That Jefferies came to his unique philosophy during the hours he spent *idly* wandering by himself each day does not undermine his knowledge or make it any less valuable. Jefferies argued for idleness, seeing it as a virtue, not that "it produces evil," but threatens those in power "because it gives time for thought, and if men had time to think their reign would come to an end."

No wonder we were taught that "the idle mind is the devil's workshop." We're supposed to be busy all our waking hours because what we might think could disrupt the existing system, and worse, be bad for business. Wild places give us an alternative to civilization, development, commerce, economic growth, threatening the status quo. No wonder we destroy them.

Toward the end of Chapter VI, Jefferies writes about the beliefs and traditions he'd grown up with. Over time, "they finally disappeared."

CHAPTER VII

～

My strength is not enough to fulfil my desire; if I had the strength of the ocean, and of the earth, the burning vigour of the sun implanted in my limbs, it would hardly suffice to gratify the measureless desire of life, which possesses me. I have often walked the day long over the sward, and, compelled to pause, at length, in my weariness, I was full of the same eagerness with which I started. The sinews would obey no longer, but the will was the same. My frame could never take the violent exertion my heart demanded. Labour of body was like meat and drink to me. Over the open hills, up the steep ascents, mile after mile, there was deep enjoyment in the long-drawn breath, the spring of the foot, in the act of rapid movement. Never have I had enough of it; I wearied long before I was satisfied, and weariness did not bring a cessation of desire; the thirst was still there.

I rowed, I used the axe, I split tree-trunks with wedges; my arms tired, but my spirit remained fresh and chafed against the physical weariness. My arms were not strong enough to satisfy me with the axe, or wedges, or oars. There was delight in the moment, but it was not enough. I swam, and what is more delicious than swimming? It is exercise and luxury at once. But

I could not swim far enough; I was always dissatisfied with myself on leaving the water. Nature has not given me a great frame, and had it done so I should still have longed for more. I was out of doors all day, and often half the night; still I wanted more sunshine, more air, the hours were too short. I feel this even more now than in the violence of early youth: the hours are too short, the day should be sixty hours long. Slumber, too, is abbreviated and restricted; forty hours of night and sleep would not be too much. So little can be accomplished in the longest summer day, so little rest and new force is accumulated in a short eight hours of sleep.

I live by the sea now; I can see nothing of it in a day; why, I do but get a breath of it, and the sun sinks before I have well begun to think. Life is so little and so mean. I dream sometimes backwards of the ancient times. If I could have the bow of Ninus, and the earth full of wild bulls and lions, to hunt them down, there would be rest in that. To shoot with a gun is nothing; a mere touch discharges it. Give me a bow, that I may enjoy the delight of feeling myself draw the string and the strong wood bending, that I may see the rush of the arrow, and the broad head bury itself deep in shaggy hide. Give me an iron mace that I may crush the savage beast and hammer him down. A spear to thrust through with, so that I may feel the long blade enter and the push of the shaft. The unwearied strength of Ninus to hunt unceasingly in the fierce sun. Still I should desire greater strength and a stouter bow, wilder creatures to combat. The intense life of the senses, there is never enough for them. I envy Semiramis; I would have been ten times Semiramis. I envy Nero, because of the great concourse of beauty he saw. I should like to be loved by every beautiful woman on earth, from the swart Nubian to the white and divine Greek.

Wine is pleasant and meat refreshing; but though I own with absolute honesty that I like them, these are the least of all. Of these two only have I ever had enough. The vehemence of exertion, the vehemence of the spear, the vehemence of sunlight and life, the insatiate desire of insatiate Semiramis, the still more insatiate desire of love, divine and beautiful, the uncontrollable adoration of beauty, these—these: give me these in greater abundance than was ever known to man or woman. The strength of Hercules, the fullness of the senses, the richness of life, would not in the least impair my desire of soul-life. On the reverse, with every stronger beat of the pulse my desire of soul-life would expand. So it has ever been with me; in hard exercise, in sensuous pleasure, in the embrace of the sunlight, even in the drinking of a glass of wine, my heart has been lifted the higher towards perfection of soul. Fullness of physical life causes a deeper desire of soul-life.

Let me be physically perfect, in shape, vigour, and movement. My frame, naturally slender, will not respond to labour, and increase in proportion to effort, nor will exposure harden a delicate skin. It disappoints me so far, but my spirit rises with the effort, and my thought opens. This is the only profit of frost, the pleasure of winter, to conquer cold, and to feel braced and strengthened by that whose province it is to wither and destroy, making of cold, life's enemy, life's renewer. The black north wind hardens the resolution as steel is tempered in ice water. It is a sensual joy, as sensuous as the warm embrace of the sunlight, but fullness of physical life ever brings to me a more eager desire of soul-life.

Splendid it is to feel the boat rise to the roller, or forced through by the sail to shear the foam aside like a share; splendid to undulate as the chest lies on the wave, swimming, the brimming ocean round: then I know and feel its deep strong tide, its immense fullness, and the sun glowing over; splendid to climb the steep green hill: in these I feel myself, I drink the exquisite joy of the senses, and my soul lifts itself with them. It is beautiful even to watch a fine horse gallop, the long stride, the rush of the wind as he passes— my heart beats quicker to the thud of the hoofs, and I feel his strength. Gladly would I have the strength of the Tartar stallion roaming the wild steppe; that very strength, what vehemence of soul-thought would accompany it. But I should like it, too, for itself. For I believe, with all my heart, in the body and the flesh, and believe that it should be increased and made more beautiful by every means. I believe—I do more than think—I believe it to be a sacred duty, incumbent upon every one, man and woman, to add to and encourage their physical life, by exercise, and in every manner. A sacred duty each towards himself, and each towards the whole of the human race. Each one of us should do some little part for the physical good of the race— health, strength, vigour. There is no harm therein to the soul: on the contrary, those who stunt their physical life are most certainly stunting their souls.

I believe all manner of asceticism to be the vilest blasphemy—blasphemy towards the whole of the human race. I believe in the flesh and the body, which is worthy of worship—to see a perfect human body unveiled causes a sense of worship. The ascetics are the only persons who are impure. Increase of physical beauty is attended by increase of soul beauty. The soul is the high even by gazing on beauty. Let me be fleshly perfect.

It is in myself that I desire increase, profit, and exaltation of body, mind, and soul. The surroundings, the clothes, the dwelling, the social status, the circumstances are to me utterly indifferent. Let the floor of the room be bare, let the furniture be a plank table, the bed a mere pallet. Let the house be plain and simple, but in the midst of air and light. These are enough—a cave would be enough; in a warmer climate the open air would suffice. Let me be furnished in myself with health, safety, strength, the perfection of physical existence; let my mind be furnished with highest thoughts of soul-life. Let me be in myself myself fully. The pageantry of power, the still more foolish pageantry of wealth, the senseless precedence of place; words fail me to express my utter contempt for such pleasure or such ambitions. Let me be in myself myself fully, and those I love equally so.

It is enough to lie on the sward in the shadow of green boughs, to listen to the songs of summer, to drink in the sunlight, the air, the flowers, the sky, the beauty of all. Or upon the hilltops to watch the white clouds rising over the curved hill-lines, their shadows descending the slope. Or on the beach to listen to the sweet sigh as the smooth sea runs up and recedes. It is lying beside the immortals, in-drawing the life of the ocean, the earth, and the sun.

I want to be always in company with these, with earth, and sun, and sea, and stars by night. The pettiness of house-life—chairs and tables—and the pettiness of observances, the petty necessity of useless labour, useless because productive of nothing, chafe me the year through. I want to be always in company with the sun, and sea, and earth. These, and the stars by night, are my natural companions. My heart looks back and sympathises with all the joy and life of ancient time. With the circling dance burned in still attitude on the vase; with the chase and the hunter eagerly pursuing, whose javelin trembles to be thrown; with the extreme fury of feeling, the whirl of joy in the warriors from Marathon to the last battle of Rome, not with the slaughter, but with the passion—the life in the passion; with the garlands and the flowers; with all the breathing busts that have panted beneath the sun. O beautiful human life! Tears come in my eyes as I think of it. So beautiful, so inexpressibly beautiful!

So deep is the passion of life that, if it were possible to live again, it must be exquisite to die pushing the eager breast against the sword. In the flush of strength to face the sharp pain joyously, and laugh in the last glance of the sun—if only to live again, now on earth, were possible. So subtle is the chord of life that sometimes to watch troops marching in rhythmic order, undulating along the column as the feet are lifted, brings tears in my eyes. Yet could I have in my own heart all the passion, the love and joy, burned in the breasts that have panted, breathing deeply, since the hour of Ilion, yet still I should desire more. How willingly I would strew the paths of all with flowers; how beautiful a delight to make the world joyous! The song should never be silent, the dance never still, the laugh should sound like water which runs for ever.

I would submit to a severe discipline, and to go without many things cheerfully, for the good and happiness of the human race in the future. Each one of us should do something, however small, towards that great end. At the present time the labour of our predecessors in this country, in all other countries of the earth, is entirely wasted. We live—that is, we snatch an existence—and our works become nothing. The piling up of fortunes, the building of cities, the establishment of immense commerce, ends in a cipher. These objects are so outside my idea that I cannot understand them, and look upon the struggle in amazement. Not even the pressure of poverty can force upon me an understanding of, and sympathy with, these things. It is the human being as the human being of whom I think. That the human being as the human being, nude—apart altogether from money, clothing, houses, properties—should enjoy greater health, strength, safety, beauty, and happiness, I would gladly agree to a discipline like that of Sparta. The Spartan method did produce the finest race of men, and Sparta was famous in antiquity for the most beautiful women. So far, therefore, it fits exactly to my ideas.

No science of modern times has yet discovered a plan to meet the requirements of the millions who live now, no plan by which they might attain similar physical proportion. Some increase of longevity, some slight improvement in the general health is promised, and these are great things, but far, far beneath the ideal. Probably the whole mode of thought of the nations must be altered before physical progress is possible. Not while money, furniture, affected show and the pageantry of wealth are the ambitions of the multitude can the multitude become ideal in form. When the ambition of the multitude is fixed on the ideal of form and beauty, then that ideal will become immediately possible, and a marked advance towards it could be made in three generations. Glad, indeed, should I be to discover something that would help towards this end.

How pleasant it would be each day to think, To-day I have done something that will tend to render future generations more happy. The very thought would make this hour sweeter. It is absolutely necessary that something of this kind should be discovered. First, we must lay down the axiom that as yet nothing has been found; we have nothing to start with; all has to be begun afresh. All courses or methods of human life have hitherto been failures. Some course of life is needed based on things that are, irrespective of tradition. The physical ideal must be kept steadily in view.

The Story of My Heart, respectively—consist mainly of thoughts and ideas that occurred to them while wandering. Their lives overlapped, and it appears that while Jefferies may have read Thoreau, Thoreau died before Jefferies wrote his best works.

Basho, the Japanese poet and haiku artist was a wanderer—

> I'm a wanderer
> so let that be my name
> the first winter rain.

Wandering is being open to the natural world. According to Thomas Heyd in his paper "Basho and the Aesthetics of Wandering,"

> Knowing nature through wandering is a process of attending to both one's own nature and the nature of one's surroundings in the particular way that they reciprocally exhibit themselves…

Back toward the house, the dogs out of sight, I drop into Placer Creek, now dry. The state of the world concerns me, specifically: am I contributing more solutions than problems? I hurry onto the flood plane which had been covered in snow all winter. Recent sun has opened a perfect path, a swath a meter wide, a dark red cut through the pure white blanket. I follow it home.

CHAPTER VIII

❧

An enumeration of the useless would almost be an enumeration of everything hitherto pursued. For instance, to go back as far as possible, the study and labour expended on Egyptian inscriptions and papyri, which contain nothing but doubtful, because laudatory, history, invocations to idols, and similar matters: all these labours are in vain. Take a broom and sweep the papyri away into the dust. The Assyrian terra-cotta tablets, some recording fables, and some even sadder—contracts between men whose bodies were dust twenty centuries since—take a hammer and demolish them. Set a battery to beat down the pyramids, and a mind-battery to destroy the deadening influence of tradition. The Greek statue lives to this day, and has the highest use of all, the use of true beauty. The Greek and Roman philosophers have the value of furnishing the mind with material to think from. Egyptian and Assyrian, mediaeval and eighteenth-century culture, miscalled, are all alike mere dust, and absolutely useless.

There is a mass of knowledge so called at the present day equally useless, and nothing but an encumbrance. We are forced by circumstances to become familiar with it, but the time expended on it is lost. No physical ideal—far less any soul-ideal—will ever be reached by it. In a recent generation, erudition in the text of the classics was considered the most honourable of pursuits; certainly nothing could be less valuable. In our own generation, another species of erudition is lauded—erudition in the laws of matter—which, in itself, is but one degree better. The study of matter for matter's sake is despicable; if any can turn that study to advance the ideal of life, it immediately becomes most valuable. But not without the human ideal. It is nothing to me if the planets revolve around the sun, or the sun around the earth, unless I can thereby gather an increase of body or mind. As the conception of the planets revolving around the sun, the present astronomical conception of the heavens is distinctly grander than that of Ptolemy; it is therefore superior, and a gain to the human mind. So with other sciences, not immediately useful, yet if they furnish the mind with material of thought, they are an advance.

But not in themselves—only in conjunction with the human ideal. Once let that slip out of the thought, and science is of no more use than the invocations in the Egyptian papyri. The world would be the gainer if the Nile rose and swept away pyramid and tomb, sarcophagus, papyri, and inscription; for it seems as if most of the superstitions which still to this hour, in our own country, hold minds in their sway, originated in Egypt. The world would be the gainer if a Nile flood of new thought arose and swept away the past, concentrating the effort of all the races of the earth upon man's body, that it might reach an ideal of shape, and health, and happiness.

Nothing is of any use unless it gives me a stronger body and mind, a more beautiful body, a happy existence, and a soul-life now. The last phase of philosophy is equally useless with the rest. The belief that the human mind was evolved, in the process of unnumbered years, from a fragment of palpitating slime through a thousand gradations, is a modern superstition, and proceeds upon assumption alone.

Nothing is evolved, no evolution takes place, there is no record of such an event; it is pure assertion. The theory fascinates many, because they find, upon study of physiology, that the gradations between animal and vegetable are so fine and so close together, as if a common web bound them together. But although they stand so near they never change places. They are like the figures on the face of a clock; there are minute dots between, apparently connecting each with the other, and the hands move round over all. Yet ten never becomes twelve, and each second even is parted from the next, as you may hear by listening to the beat. So the gradations of life, past and present, though standing close together never change places. Nothing is evolved. There is no evolution any more than there is any design in nature. By standing face to face with nature, and not from books, I have convinced myself that there is no design and no evolution. What there is, what was the cause, how and why, is not yet known; certainly it was neither of these.

But it may be argued the world must have been created, or it must have been made of existing things, or it must have been evolved, or it must have existed for ever, through all eternity. I think not. I do not think that either of these are "musts," nor that any "must" has yet been discovered; not even that there "must" be a first cause. There may be other things— other physical forces even—of which we know nothing. I strongly suspect there are. There may be other ideas altogether from any we have hitherto had the use of. For many ages our ideas have been confined to two or three. We have conceived the idea of creation, which is the highest and grandest of all, if not historically true; we have conceived the idea of design, that is of an intelligence making order and revolution of chaos; and we have conceived the idea of evolution by physical laws of matter, which, though now so much insisted on, is as ancient as the Greek philosophers. But there may be another alternative; I think there are other alternatives.

Whenever the mind obtains a wider view, we may find that origin, for instance, is not always due to what is understood by cause. At this moment the mind is unable to conceive of anything happening, or of anything coming into existence, without a cause. From cause to effect is the sequence of our ideas. But I think that if at some time we should obtain an altogether different

and broader sequence of ideas, we may discover that
there are various other alternatives. As the world, and
the universe at large, was not constructed according to
plan, so it is clear that the sequence or circle of ideas,
which includes plan, and cause, and effect, are not in
the circle of ideas, which would correctly explain it.
Put aside the plan-circle of ideas, and it will at once be
evident that there is no inherent necessity or "must."
There is no inherent necessity for a first cause, or that
the world and the universe was created, or that it was
shaped of existing matter, or that it evolved itself and
its inhabitants, or that the cosmos has existed in vary-
ing forms forever. There may be other alternatives altogether. The only idea I can give is the idea that there
is another idea.

In this "must"—"it must follow"—lies my objec-
tion to the logic of science. The arguments proceed
from premises to conclusions, and end with the assumption "it therefore follows." But I say that, however
carefully the argument be built up, even though apparently flawless, there is no such thing at present as "it
must follow." Human ideas at present naturally form
a plan, and a balanced design; they might be indicated
by a geometrical figure, an upright straight line in the
centre, and branching from that straight line curves
on either hand exactly equal to each other. In draw-
ing that is how we are taught, to balance the outline
or curves on one side with the curves on the other. In
nature and in fact there is no such thing. The stem of

a tree represents the upright line, but the branches do not balance; those on one side are larger or longer than those on the other. Nothing is straight, but all things curved, crooked, and unequal.

The human body is the most remarkable instance of inequality, lack of balance, and want of plan. The exterior is beautiful in its lines, but the two hands, the two feet, the two sides of the face, the two sides of the profile, are not precisely equal. The very nails of the fingers are set ajar, as it were, to the lines of the hand, and not quite straight. Examination of the interior organs shows a total absence of balance. The heart is not in the centre, nor do the organs correspond in any way. The viscera are wholly opposed to plan. Coming, lastly, to the bones, these have no humanity, as it were, of shape; they are neither round nor square; the first sight of them causes a sense of horror, so extra-human are they in shape; there is no balance of design in them. These are very brief examples, but the whole universe, so far as it can be investigated, is equally unequal. No straight line runs through it, with balanced curves each side.

Let this thought now be carried into the realms of thought. The mind, or circle, or sequence of ideas, acts, or thinks, or exists in a balance, or what seems a balance to it. A straight line of thought is set in the centre, with equal branches each side, and with a generally rounded outline. But this corresponds to nothing in tangible fact. Hence I think, by analogy, we may suppose that neither does it correspond to the circle of ideas which caused us and all things to be, or, at all events, to the circle of ideas which accurately understand us and all things. There are other ideas altogether. From standing face to face so long with the real earth, the real sun, and the real sea, I am firmly convinced that there is an immense range of thought quite unknown to us yet.

The problem of my own existence also convinces me that there is much more. The questions are: Did my soul exist before my body was formed? Or did it come into life with my body, as a product, like a flame, of combustion? What will become of it after death? Will it simply go out like a flame and become non-existent, or will it live forever in one or other mode? To these questions I am unable to find any answer whatsoever. In our present range of ideas there is no reply to them. I may have previously existed; I may not have previously existed. I may be a product of combustion; I may exist on after physical life is suspended, or I may not. No demonstration is possible. But what I want to say is that the alternatives of extinction or immortality may not be the only alternatives. There may be something else, more wonderful than immortality, and far beyond and above that idea. There may be something immeasurably superior to it. As our ideas have run in circles for centuries, it is difficult to find words to express the idea that there are other ideas. For myself, though I cannot fully express myself, I feel fully convinced that there is a vast immensity of thought, of existence, and of other things beyond even immortal existence.

EVOLUTION

Opinions of those who've read *The Story of My Heart* cover the full spectrum from love to disdain. I'm most interested in those who disliked it intensely and those whom it completely inspired.

W.H. Hudson, British author, naturalist, and ornithologist, best known for his exotic romances, especially *Green Mansions*, found *The Story of My Heart* embarrassing and bordering on insanity.

Harold Massingham, a prolific Brit who wrote about the English countryside and agriculture and was also a poet, found *The Story of My Heart* to be "a thoroughly bad book—utterly chaotic, full of contradictions and repetitions, lacking in artistry, the morbid outpourings of a sick and disappointed man."

Malcolm Elwin, twentieth-century British biographer and critic, suggested that Jefferies had character defects brought on by an unhappy home life and professional failures. Elwin felt that his neurotic personality, morbidity and "sick mind" turned *The Story of My Heart* into a "dithyramb of emotional torment… full of platitudes, repetition, loose and nonsensical expressions."

I had to look up *dithyramb* to feel the full force of Elwin's venom. It means "a passionate or inflated speech, poem, or other writing."

More recently, Colin Laurie McKelvie, a British

naturalist, found *The Story of My Heart* "a flawed and unsatisfactory text, which borders on incoherence," which rambles and is "barely comprehensible."

H.M. Tomlinson, the London-based writer known for anti-war novels and short stories, called *The Story of My Heart* "a dangerous book."

In contrast, there are other writers who praise Jefferies and *The Story of My Heart* for its radical insights and inspiration of what it means to be a human being engaged in the world.

John Fowles, the Englishman who wrote *The Collector*, *The Tree*, and *The French Lieutenant's Woman*, cites Richard Jefferies as an intellectual mentor along with Camus and Sartre. Fowles wrote an introduction to Jefferies' novel, *After London*, in which a huge winter storm wreaks death and destruction on the city, not so far-fetched with the recent Polar Vortex experienced in the United States. "His prose," Fowles writes, referring to Jefferies, "is like nature itself."

We only recently discovered that Rachel Carson, perhaps Terry's longest and most pronounced source of inspiration, always kept *Walden* and *The Story of My Heart* on her bedside table.

Henry Williamson read *The Story of My Heart* in 1919 when he was twenty-three. He considered Jefferies his "great mentor." He felt the book to be nothing short of "the most beautiful and noble book in the world." Williamson was also an inspiration to Rachel Carson. We won't go into his comparing Jefferies to

Hitler and Jesus, both of whom he viewed as "prophets crying, and perishing in the industrial wilderness of the gold-god civilization."

Henry Salt wrote extensively of Jefferies, including the classic *Richard Jefferies: His Life & his Ideals* (1894) in which he compares *The Story of My Heart* to Thoreau's *Walden*.

Henry Miller—yes that Henry Miller—known for breaking traditional literary forms, for his explicit language, sex, mysticism, and his banned books, wrote in his essay "Books in My Life," "Here is a man [Jefferies!] who speaks my inmost thoughts." Miller felt he lacked Jefferies' courage and honesty, saying that truly inspirational writers —like Jefferies—don't force new beliefs upon us, but help us "penetrate reality more deeply, to make progress in the science of reality." I love this. "They point to something beyond thought, to the ocean of mind, let us say, in which thought swims." Jefferies, Miller believes, reminds us that the natural world is the source of these ideas, which "never will dry up."

Why such contrast between Jefferies' detractors and his disciples? Could it be as simple as experience? Those who think him insane have never had the—call them transcendental—experiences that he and his disciples had, experiences that until Jefferies put words to them, were thought to be eternally ineffable? Or this could be simply that there are those who regularly wander in the wilds, and those who don't.

Richard Jefferies and I share obsessions—wildness as the source of true knowledge, wandering as access to that knowledge. We also share experiences, which have more meaning now that I've read his words. Beyond that, Jefferies saves me by giving me courage to write without caring who might ever read what I've written.

When I began this chapter, I was definitely in the Jefferies-has-completely-inspired-me camp. But the first few pages made me question that. Jefferies seems frustrated here. He sees no value in anything, even the planets revolving around the sun, unless it can "advance the ideal of life." He sees everything through the limited lens of the "human ideal." This human-centered philosophy may be the thickest root of our most severe problems, I thought as I scrambled to rationalize what Jefferies wrote.

"Nothing is of use unless it gives me a stronger body and mind, a more beautiful body, a happy existence, and a soul-life now." This may be due to his own debilitating disease that would eventually kill him.[2]

---

2. In *Richard Jefferies: His Life and Work*, Edward Thomas discovered that Jefferies began taking notes for *The Story of My Heart* in 1880. "In December, 1881, Jefferies fell ill of fistula, perhaps tubercular in origin, and during the next twelve months four times suffered the painful operation which is used to cure this disease: 'the pain,' he wrote, 'was awful—like lightening through the brain', but he was not prostrate or unable to work for the whole of this time...The wounds were not all healed until January, 1883. Within a month he began to feel a gnawing internal pain; it was, he said, like the gnawing of a rat at a beam, or the burning of corrosive sublimate. He feared

Later, reading what Jefferies wrote about evolution, I panicked, thinking that this may become our irreconcilable difference.

Jefferies is adamant about the impossibility that something as sophisticated as the human mind has over eons developed from "a fragment of palpitating slime…Nothing is evolved, no evolution takes place, there is no record of such an event; it is pure assertion."

I bristled when I read that, and I'm bristling now writing this, although less so. Once I finished the chapter and looked for context for what I'd read, I find myself, after a series of discoveries, somewhat transformed.

First, Darwin is one of my heroes. I've read nearly everything by or about him, and I believe what I've read. Darwin and my great-great-great-grandfather grew up in the same town at the same time.

Jefferies might be exhibiting professional jealousy. I can't find if he read any of Darwin's books, but he could have—they were all available to him: *The Voyage of the Beagle* was published in 1839; *The Origin of Species* in 1859; *The Descent of Man* in 1871. As a naturalist, Jefferies may have envied Darwin's ability to travel the world. The youthful Jefferies launched two failed attempts to see the world, one to Russia and the other

---

travel by train lest he should throw himself out." But, "On June 22, 1883, Jefferies wrote to say that he had just finished writing a book about which he had been meditating seventeen years; he had called it *The Story of My Heart: An Autobiography*."

to America, but never got very far. Jefferies may have wondered what he might have accomplished with Darwin's resources—Darwin came from a wealthy family and never really needed to work. Jefferies' violent and, I believe, unreasonable reaction to evolution suggests that he was jealous of Darwin. I might be wrong.

Morris argues that Jefferies "explicitly distanced himself from Darwin" which suggests that Jefferies knew something about him. Morris also notes that Jefferies attributed Lamarck as having a significant influence on his Nature philosophy.

Lamarck, I remembered from college, is the French biologist known for his theory of how species evolve by passing acquired characteristics from one generation to the next—the use/disuse theory. Lamarckian evolution was illustrated by the giraffe's long neck: rather than a long period of natural selection, one giraffe stretched its neck in one generation in order to reach the leaves high on a tree. That long neck was passed on to the next generation, and so on.

Midway through this chapter, Jefferies writes about being limited by our ideas as if they are finite, that if our mind ever "obtains a wider view" alternatives may be possible. He's referring to the sequence of ideas regarding species through time—from creation to design, and now evolution "which though now so much insisted on, is as ancient as the Greek Philosophers."

"The only idea I can give is that there is another

idea," Jefferies offers, suggesting we make a mistake by assuming that we know everything, that there are no new ideas. But, if we stand wild, "face to face so long with the real earth, the real sun, the real sea," we may also be "firmly convinced that there is an immense range of thought quite unknown to us yet." Our main problem may be thinking that all major discoveries have been made and solving problems is a simple matter of bringing different elements of our knowledge together in the right combination. With climate change, this may spell disaster, as experts believe that successfully dealing with it will require all that we now know and a lot we don't yet know.

Recent discoveries show that a new concept known as epigenetics has breathed new life into the previously discredited Lamarckian theory of evolution.

In a 2009 article, "A Comeback for Lamarckian Evolution," Emily Singer examined the surprising results of two tests, which showed that the effects of a mother's early environment can be passed on to her offspring. The studies were done on mice, but if the results can be applied to humans, the research suggests that both childhood education and abuse can impact future generations. In other words, characteristics acquired by a young girl can later affect her children.

Although recent findings don't explain the giraffe neck length, epigenetics is indeed a form of *soft inheritance.*

"The only idea I have is that there is another idea."

Jefferies personalizes this, wonders where he came from, where he's going. I love his questions. He knows—consciously or not—that he's not long for the world. He wonders about whether his soul existed before he was born or "did it come into life with my body, as a product, *like a flame, of combustion?*"

"Terry, please. Read that again," I remember saying. We were in Maine, sitting in big wooden chairs just before sunset. Small reddish dragonflies hunted gnats while we took turns, one of us reading a chapter while the other watched for the red fox that often passed through that time of night. "Like a flame, of *combustion*," she read again. It was a moment I marked.

When he dies will his soul die with his body, going "out like a flame" or will it go on? "*I may be a product of combustion; I may exist on after physical life is suspended, or I may not.*"

"There may be other alternatives," he suggests, something better than even immortality. He would be dead in five years.

CHAPTER IX

⁓

In human affairs, everything happens by chance—that is, in defiance of human ideas, and without any direction of an intelligence. A man bathes in a pool, a crocodile seizes and lacerates his flesh. If anyone maintains that an intelligence directed that cruelty, I can only reply that his mind is under an illusion. A man is caught by a revolving shaft and torn to pieces, limb from limb. There is no directing intelligence in human affairs, no protection, and no assistance. Those who act uprightly are not rewarded, but they and their children often wander in the utmost indigence. Those who do evil are not always punished, but frequently flourish and have happy children. Rewards and punishments are purely human institutions, and if government be relaxed they entirely disappear. No intelligence whatever interferes in human affairs. There is a most senseless belief now prevalent that effort, and work, and cleverness, perseverance and industry, are invariably successful. Were this the case, every man would enjoy a competence, at least, and be free from the cares of money. This is an illusion almost equal to the superstition of a directing intelligence, which every fact and every consideration disproves.

How can I adequately express my contempt for

the assertion that all things occur for the best, for a wise and beneficent end, and are ordered by a humane intelligence! It is the most utter falsehood and a crime against the human race. Even in my brief time I have been contemporary with events of the most horrible character; as when the mothers in the Balkans cast their own children from the train to parish in the snow; as when the Princess Alice foundered, and six hundred human beings were smothered in foul water; as when the hecatomb of two thousand maidens were burned in the church at Santiago; as when the miserable creatures tore at the walls of the Vienna theatre. Consider only the fates, which overtake the little children. Human suffering is so great, so endless, so awful that I can hardly write of it. I could not go into hospitals and face it, as some do, lest my mind should be temporarily overcome. The whole and the worst the worst pessimist can say is far beneath the least particle of the truth, so immense is the misery of man. It is the duty of all rational beings to acknowledge the truth. There is not the least trace of directing intelligence in human affairs. This is a foundation of hope, because, if the present condition of things were ordered by a superior power, there would be no possibility of improving it for the better in the spite of that power. Acknowledging that no such direction exists, all things become at once plastic to our will.

The credit given by the unthinking to the statement that all affairs are directed has been the bane of the world since the days of the Egyptian papyri and the origin of superstition. So long as men firmly believe that everything is fixed for them, so long is progress impossible. If you argue yourself into the belief that you cannot walk to a place, you cannot walk there. But if you start you can walk there easily. Anyone who will consider the affairs of the world at large, and of the individual, will see that they do not proceed in the manner they would do for our own happiness if a man of humane breadth of view were placed at their head with unlimited power, such as is credited to the intelligence which does not exist. A man of intellect and humanity could cause everything to happen in an infinitely superior manner. Could one like the divine Julius—humane, generous, broadest of view, deep thinking—wield such power, certainly, every human being would enjoy happiness.

But that which is thoughtlessly credited to a nonexistent intelligence should really be claimed and exercised by the human race. It is ourselves who should direct our affairs, protecting ourselves from pain, assisting ourselves, succouring and rendering our lives happy. We must do for ourselves what superstition has hitherto supposed an intelligence to do for us. Nothing whatsoever is done for us. We are born naked, and not even protected by a shaggy covering. Nothing is done for us. The first and strongest command (using the word to convey the idea only) that nature, the universe, our own bodies give, is to do everything for ourselves. The sea does not make boats for us, nor the earth of her own will build us hospitals. The injured lie bleeding, and no invisible power lifts them up. The maidens were scorched in the midst of their devotions, and their remains make a mound hundreds of yards long. The infants perished in the snow, and the ravens tore their limbs. Those in the theatre crushed each other to the death—agony. For how long, for how many thousand years, must the earth and the sea, and the fire and the air, utter these things and force them upon us before they are admitted in their full significance?

These things speak with a voice of thunder. From every human being whose body has been racked by pain; from every human being who has suffered from accident or disease; from every human being drowned, burned, or slain by negligence, there goes up a continually increasing cry louder than the thunder. An awe-inspiring cry dread to listen to, which no one dares listen to, against which ears are stopped by the wax of superstition and the wax of criminal selfishness: These miseries are your doing, because you have mind and thought, and could have prevented them. You can prevent them in the future. You do not even try.

It is perfectly certain that all diseases without exception are preventable, or, if not so, that they can be so weakened as to do no harm. It is perfectly certain that all accidents are preventable; there is not one that does not arise from folly or negligence. All accidents

are crimes. It is perfectly certain that all human beings are capable of physical happiness. It is absolutely
incontrovertible that the ideal shape of the human being is attainable to the exclusion of deformities. It is
incontrovertible that there is no necessity for any man
to die but of old age, and that if death cannot be prevented life can be prolonged far beyond the farthest
now known. It is incontrovertible that at the present
time no one ever dies of old age. Not one single person
ever dies of old age, or of natural causes, for there is no
such thing as a natural cause of death. They die of disease or weakness, which is the result of disease either
in themselves or in their ancestors. No such thing as
old age is known to us. We do not even know what old
age would be like, because no one ever lives to it.

Our bodies are full of unsuspected flaws, handed
down it may be for thousands of years, and it is of
these that we die, and not of natural decay. Till these
are eliminated, or as nearly eliminated as possible, we
shall never even know what true old age is like, nor
what the true natural limit of human life is. The utmost
limit now appears to be about one hundred and five
years, but as each person who has got so far has died
of weaknesses inherited through thousands of years, it
is impossible to say to what number of years he would
have reached in a natural state. It seems more than
possible that true old age—the slow and natural decay
of the body apart from inherited flaw—would be free
from very many, if not all, of the petty miseries, which

now render extreme age a doubtful blessing. If the limbs grew weaker they would not totter; if the teeth dropped it would not be till the last; if the eyes were less strong they would not be quite dim; nor would the mind lose its memory.

But now we see eyes become dim and artificial aid needed in comparative youth, and teeth drop out in mere childhood. Many men and women lose teeth before they are twenty. This simple fact is evidence enough of inherited weakness or flaw. How could a person who had lost teeth before twenty be ever said to die of old age, though he died at a hundred and ten? Death is not a supernatural event; it is an event of the most materialistic character, and may certainly be postponed, by the united efforts of the human race, to a period far more distant from the date of birth than has been the case during the historic period. The question has often been debated in my mind whether death is or is not wholly preventable; whether, if the entire human race were united in their efforts to eliminate causes of decay, death might not also be altogether eliminated.

If we consider ourselves by the analogy of animals, trees, and other living creatures, the reply is that, however postponed, in long process of time the tissues must wither. Suppose an ideal man, free from inherited flaw, then though his age might be prolonged to several centuries, in the end the natural body must wear out. That is true so far. But it so happens that the analogy is not just, and therefore the conclusions it points to are not tenable.

Man is altogether different from every other animal, every other living creature known. He is different in body. In his purely natural state—in his true natural state—he is immeasurably stronger. No animal approaches to the physical perfection of which a man is capable. He can weary the strongest horse, he can outrun the swiftest stag, he can bear extremes of heat and cold hunger and thirst, which would exterminate every known living thing. Merely in bodily strength he is superior to all. The stories of antiquity, which were deemed fables, may be fables historically, but search has shown that they are not intrinsically fables. Man of flesh and blood is capable of all that Ajax, all that Hercules did. Feats in modern days have surpassed these, as when Webb swam the Channel; mythology contains nothing equal to that. The difference does not end here. Animals think to a certain extent, but if their conceptions be ever so clever, not having hands they cannot execute them.

I myself maintain that the mind of man is practically infinite. It can understand anything brought before it. It has not the power of its own motion to bring everything before it, but when anything is brought it is understood. It is like sitting in a room with one window; you cannot compel everything to pass the window, but whatever does pass is seen. It is like a magnifying glass, which magnifies and explains everything brought into its focus. The mind of man is infinite. Beyond this, man has a soul. I do not use this word in the common sense which circumstances have given to it. I use it as the only term to express that inner consciousness which aspires. These brief reasons show that the analogy is imperfect, and that therefore, although an ideal animal—a horse, a dog, a lion—must die, it does not follow that an ideal man must. He has a body possessed of exceptional recuperative powers, which, under proper conditions, continually repairs itself. He has a mind by which he can select remedies, and select his course and carefully restore the waste of tissue. He has a soul, as yet, it seems to me, lying in abeyance, by the aid of which he may yet discover things now deemed supernatural.

Considering these things, I am obliged by facts and incontrovertible argument to conclude that death is not inevitable to the ideal man. He is shaped for a species of physical immortality. The beauty of form of the ideal human being indicates immortality—the contour, the curve, the outline answer to the idea of life. In the course of ages united effort long continued may eliminate those causes of decay which have grown up in ages past, and after that has been done advance farther and improve the natural state. As a river brings down suspended particles of sand, and depositing them at its mouth forms a delta and a new country; as the air and the rain and the heat of the sun desiccate the rocks and slowly wear down mountains into sand, so the united action of the human race, continued through centuries, may build up the ideal man and woman. Each individual labouring in his day through geological time in front must produce an effect. The instance of Sparta, where so much was done in a few centuries, is almost proof of it.

The truth is, we die through our ancestors; we are murdered by our ancestors. Their dead hands stretch forth from the tomb and drag us down to their mouldering bones. We in our turn are now at this moment preparing death for our unborn posterity. This day those that die do not die in the sense of old age, they are slain. Nothing has been accumulated for our benefit in ages past. All the labour and the toil of so many millions continued through such vistas of time, down to those millions who at this hour are rushing to and fro in London, has accumulated nothing for us. Nothing for our good. The only things that have been stored up have been for our evil and destruction, diseases and weaknesses crossed and cultivated and rendered almost part and parcel of our very bones. Now let us begin to roll back the tide of death, and to set our faces steadily to a future of life. It should be the sacred and sworn duty of every one, once at least during lifetime, to do something in person towards this end. It would be a delight and pleasure to me to do something every day, were it ever so minute. To reflect that another human being, if at a distance of ten thousand years from the year 1883, would enjoy one hour's more life, in the sense of fullness of life, in consequence of anything I had done in my little span, would be to me a peace of soul.

IMMORTALITY

Last week, back together in Jackson, Terry and I watched the film *Love in the Time of Cholera*, which we loved nearly as much as the book by Gabriel Garcia Marquez. Lately I pass everything through my Richard Jefferies filter—no surprise that the phrase from the film, "our inner lives are immortal" stuck. To get a better sense of the context, I looked up the line in the book. Marquez, I discovered, actually wrote, "our inner lives are eternal, which is to say that our spirits remain as youthful, as vigorous as when we were in full bloom." Why would the screenwriter substitute *immortal* for *eternal*? As Mormon kids growing up, we were promised eternal life if we passed a few tests, lived by some rules. Life was intended to be tough and suffering was part of it. We were taught to endure to the end. If we died "worthy" we'd go to paradise until the resurrection, when we would rise physically from the grave. I remember the childhood image of sitting up in the grave, brushing away the dirt, standing up and stretching.

For us, the closest thing we had to an "inner life" was the "still small voice" of the Holy Ghost, who would whisper in our ears, telling us what we should do.

I took those "promptings" seriously and when presented with two options as an alternative to being drafted for the Vietnam War, chose the Army Reserve rather than a Mormon mission. An eighteen-year-old

Mormon kid one day, I found myself in basic training learning to kill people the next. I thought a lot about death and immortality.

"Beyond immortality" is a recurring theme for Jefferies.

Why Jefferies' obsession? Was he sensing his own death? Was he worried that "immortality" meant he might continue suffering forever? Something beyond immortality held more promise.

In the last few months of his illness, unable to be outside with nature, Jefferies "turned inward and became more metaphysical."[3] Jefferies sent letters[4] to a friend in which he described himself as "the veriest shadow of a man, like a living man tied to a dead one, mind alive and body dead."

Jefferies believed that for the ideal man, "death is not inevitable." He believed that beyond immortality this ideal man would discover "things now deemed supernatural."

But then, this ideal and potentially infinite man dies "through our ancestors; we are murdered by our ancestors."

Is Jefferies writing in general as well as personal

---

3. Looker, perhaps Jefferies' most intense disciple, published in *The Nature Diaries and Notebooks of Richard Jefferies* transcriptions of dozens of the journals Jefferies kept (in handwriting more horrible than mine) between 1881 and 1883, hoping for insights into how he felt and what he may have been thinking. I found reminders of what a poet Jefferies was, when he wasn't trying. My favorite: Daglets Icicles as bare as a toad of feathers.

4. H.S. Salt, in his book, *Richard Jeffries: His Life & His Ideals*

terms, referring to his own illness (his anal fistula[5], his tuberculosis, etc.) as hereditary, passed down from his ancestors?

> Their dead hands stretch forth from the tomb and drag us down to their mouldering bones. We in turn are now at this moment preparing death for our unborn posterity. This day those that die do not die in the sense of old age, they are slain.

Quantum physicists contend that our physical death is but a blip in our total existence, that the soul or consciousness is information stored at the quantum level where it merges with our universe and might exist there indefinitely.

Robert Pogue Harrison in his book *The Dominion of the Dead*, says "that we follow in the footsteps of the dead…Whether we are conscious of it or not we do the will of the ancestors." Harrison says the dead have a close relationship with the unborn, that

> The former hound the living with guilt, dread, and a sense of responsibility, obliging us, by whatever means necessary, to take the unborn into our care and to keep the story going, even if we never quite know what the story is about, what our part in it is, the end toward which it is progressing, or the moral it contains.

---

5. H.S. Salt reported that the details of Jefferies' illness "are so harrowing in their intensity that his biographer 'dared not quote the whole of this dreadful story of long-continued agony,'…"

To keep the story going.

Opening *The Story of My Heart* that first time was opening a door between the living and the dead, between this world and that. Had I been listening, I might have heard Jefferies saying, "Ok, good. I've been looking for someone new to move this forward. It's getting serious out there."

If the living inherit obsessions, burdens, and causes from the dead, then by becoming my obsession, Jefferies is immortal, continuing through me the work he engaged in during life.

But what about "immortal," the word used synonymously with "eternal," the word Terry and I grew up with?

Mormons believe that all life is immortal because Christ sacrificed for everyone and everything, that immortality doesn't require obedience. But eternal life, the greatest gift, comes only after strict adherence to all gospel principles, jumping through all the Mormon hoops of ritual, and "enduring to the end." Mormons believe that for those who are worthy, eternal life is living the life of God, with God. Living a God-like life. Being gods of their own universes.

If everyone and every living thing becomes immortal, but only those deemed worthy can be eternal, then eternal life is "beyond Immortality"—what Jefferies longed for. I can only imagine that, had he lived long enough for the Mormon missionaries to find his house, he might have let them baptize him once they'd said, "Yes, Brother Jefferies, there is something beyond immortality and it is the Eternal Life we offer you."

"Holy shit," I say out loud, taking a deep breath. I think about what might have happened had Jefferies lived to a ripe old age. He could have achieved cosmic consciousness. Or he might have converted to Mormonism. Hell, he might have come to Salt Lake City, having discovered what is "beyond immortality."

We tell stories about things we can never really know. Perhaps the Mormon story about eternity and mine aren't all that different—separated only by our idea of where God actually dwells.

Terry and I talked about the Mormon difference between immortal and eternal, and that long-ago spring dawn when we frisbeed the plate adorned with the Salt Lake Temple out into the Great Salt Lake, our "eternal" marriage flying off with it, shattering in the salt-dense water. Although we didn't know it at the time, we opted for *immortal* with everything else alive. We gambled a straight, paved, well-lit *eternal* path for one rugged and unknown, comfortable knowing that part of being human is finding peace with uncertainty. We still don't know where we're headed. We do know that when we're quiet and alone in the wilds, a force surfaces from deep in our bones, moving us toward something right, something good.

CHAPTER X

~

United effort through geological time in front is but the beginning of an idea. I am convinced that much more can be done, and that the length of time may be almost immeasurably shortened. The general principles that are now in operation are of the simplest and most elementary character, yet they have already made considerable difference. I am not content with these. There must be much more—there must be things which are at present unknown by whose aid advance may be made. Research proceeds upon the same old lines and runs in the ancient grooves. Further, it is restricted by the ultra-practical views, which are alone deemed reasonable. But there should be no limit placed on the mind. The purely ideal is as worthy of pursuit as the practical, and the mind is not to be pinned to dogmas of science any more than to dogmas of superstition. Most injurious of all is the continuous circling on the same path, and it is from this that I wish to free my mind.

The pursuit of theory—the organon of pure thought—has led incidentally to great discoveries, and for myself I am convinced it is of the highest value. The process of experiment has produced much, and has applied what was previously found. Empiricism is worthy of careful re-working out, for it is a fact that most things are more or less empirical, especially in medicine. Denial may be given to this statement, nevertheless it is true, and I have had practical exemplification of it in my own experience. Observation is perhaps more powerful an organon than either experiment or empiricism. If the eye is always watching, and the mind on the alert, ultimately chance supplies the solution.

The difficulties I have encountered have generally been solved by chance in this way. When I took an interest in archaeological matters—an interest long since extinct—I considered that a part of an army known to have marched in a certain direction during the Civil War must have visited a town in which I was interested. But I exhausted every mode of research in vain; there was no evidence of it. If the knowledge had ever existed it had dropped again. Some years afterwards, when my interest had ceased, and I had put such inquiries for ever aside (being useless, like the Egyptian papyri), I was reading in the British Museum. Presently I returned my book to the shelf, and then slowly walked along the curving wall lined with volumes, looking to see if I could light on anything to amuse me. I took out a volume for a glance; it opened of itself at a certain page, and there was the information I had so long sought—a reprint of an old pamphlet describing the visit of the army to the town in the Civil War. So chance answered the question in the course of time.

And I think that, seeing how great a part chance plays in human affairs, it is essential that study should be made of chance; it seems to me that an organon from experiment. Then there is the inner consciousness—the psyche—that has never yet been brought to bear upon life and its questions. Besides which there is a super-sensuous reason. Often I have argued with myself that such and such a course was the right one to follow, while in the intervals of thinking about it an undercurrent of unconscious impulse has desired me to do the reverse or to remain inactive. Sometimes it has happened that the super-sensuous reasoning has been correct, and the most faultless argument wrong. I presume this super-sensuous reasoning, preceeding independently in the mind, arises from perceptions too delicate for analysis. From these considerations alone I am convinced that, by the aid of ideas yet to be discovered, the geological time in front may be immeasurably shortened. These modes of research are not all. The psyche—the soul in me—tells me that there is much more, that these are merely beginnings of the crudest kind.

I fully recognise the practical difficulty arising from the ingrained, hereditary, and unconscious selfishness, which began before history, and has been crossed and cultivated for twelve thousand years since. This renders me less sanguine of united effort through geological time ahead, unless some idea can be formed to give a stronger impulse even than selfishness, or unless the selfishness can be utilised. The complacency with which the mass of people go about their daily task, absolutely indifferent to all other considerations, is appalling in its concentrated stolidity. They do not intend wrong—they intend rightly: in truth, they work against the entire human race. So wedded and so confirmed is the world in its narrow groove of self, so stolid and so complacent under the immense weight of misery, so callous to its own possibilities, and so grown to its chains, that I almost despair to see it awakened. Cemeteries are often placed on hillsides, and the white stones are visible far off. If the whole of the dead in a hillside cemetery were called up alive from their tombs, and walked forth down into the valley, it would not rouse the mass of people from the dense pyramid of stolidity which presses on them.

There would be gaping and marvelling and rushing about, and what then? In a week or two the ploughman would settle down to his plough, the carpenter to his bench, the smith to his anvil, the merchant to his money, and the dead come to life would be utterly forgotten. No matter in what manner the possibilities of human life are put before the world, the crowd continues as stolid as before. Therefore, nothing hitherto done, or suggested, or thought of, is of much avail; but this fact in no degree stays me from the search. On the contrary, the less there has been accomplished the more anxious I am; the truth it teaches is that the mind must be lifted out of its old grooves before anything will be certainly begun. Erase the past from the mind—stand face to face with the real now—and work out all anew. Call the soul to our assistance; the soul tells me that outside all the ideas that have yet occurred there are others, whole circles of others.

I remember a cameo of Augustus Caesar—the head of the emperor is graven in delicate lines, and shows the most exquisite proportions. It is a balanced head, a head adjusted to the calmest intellect. That head when it was living contained a circle of ideas, the largest, the widest, the most profound current in his time. All that philosophy had taught, all that practice, experiment, and empiricism had discovered, was familiar to him. There was no knowledge in the ancient world but what was accessible to the Emperor of Rome. Now at this day there are amongst us heads as finely proportioned as that cut out in the cameo. Though these living men do not possess arbitrary power, the advantages of arbitrary power—as far as knowledge is concerned—are secured to them by education, by the printing-press, and the facilities of our era. It is reasonable to imagine a head of our time filled with the largest, the widest, the most profound ideas current in the age. Augustus Caesar, however great his intellect, could not in that balanced head have possessed the ideas familiar enough to the living head of this day. As we have a circle of ideas unknown to Augustus Caesar, so I argue there are whole circles of ideas unknown to us. It is these that I am so earnestly desirous of discovering.

For nothing has as yet been of any value, however good its intent. There is no virtue, or reputed virtue, which has not been rigidly pursued, and things have remained as before. Men and women have practised self-denial, and to what end? They have compelled themselves to suffer hunger and thirst; in vain. They have clothed themselves in sackcloth and lacerated the flesh. They have mutilated themselves. Some have been scrupulous to bathe, and some have been scrupulous to cake their bodies with the foulness of years. Many have devoted their lives to assist others in sickness or poverty. Chastity has been faithfully observed, chastity both of body and mind. Self-examination has been pursued till it ended in a species of sacred insanity, and all these have been of no more value than the tortures undergone by the Indian mendicant who hangs himself up by a hook through his back. All these are pure folly.

Asceticism has not improved the form, or the physical well-being, or the heart of any human being. On the contrary, the hetaira is often the warmest hearted and the most generous. Casuistry and self-examination are perhaps the most injurious of all the virtues, utterly destroying independence of mind. Self-denial has had no result, and all the self-torture of centuries has been thrown away. Lives spent in doing good have been lives nobly wasted. Everything is in vain. The circle of ideas we possess is too limited to aid us. We need ideas as far outside our circle as ours are outside those that were pondered over by Augustus Caesar.

The most extraordinary spectacle, as it seems to me, is the vast expenditure of labour and time wasted in obtaining mere subsistence. As a man, in his lifetime, works hard and saves money, that his children may be free from the cares of penury and may at least have sufficient to eat, drink, clothe, and roof them, so the generations that preceded us might, had they so chosen, have provided for our subsistence. The labour and time of ten generations, properly directed, would sustain a hundred generations succeeding to them, and that, too, with so little self-denial on the part of the providers as to be scarcely felt. So men now, in this generation, ought clearly to be laying up a store, or, what is still more powerful, arranging and organising that the generations which follow may enjoy comparative freedom from useless labour. Instead of which, with transcendent improvidence, the world works only for today, as the world worked twelve thousand years ago, and our children's children will still have to toil and slave for the bare necessities of life. This is, indeed an extraordinary spectacle.

That twelve thousand written years should have elapsed, and the human race—able to reason and to think, and easily capable of combination in immense armies for its own destruction—should still live from hand to mouth, like cattle and sheep, like the animals of the field and the birds of the woods; that there should not even be roofs to cover the children born, unless those children labour and expend their time to pay for them; that there should not be clothes, unless, again, time and labour are expended to procure them; that there should not be even food for the children of the human race, except they labour as their fathers did twelve thousand years ago; that even water should scarce be accessible to them, unless paid for by labour! In twelve thousand written years the world has not yet built itself a House, nor filled a Granary, nor organised itself for its own comfort. It is so marvellous I cannot express the wonder with which it fills me. And more wonderful still, if that could be, there are people so infatuated, or, rather, so limited of view, that they glory in this state of things, declaring that work is the main object of man's existence—work for subsistence—and glorying in their wasted time. To argue with such is impossible; to leave them is the only resource.

This our earth this day produces sufficient for our existence. This our earth produces not only a sufficiency, but a superabundance, and pours a cornucopia of good things down upon us. Further, it produces sufficient for stores and granaries to be filled to the roof-tree for years ahead. I verily believe that the earth in one year produces enough food to last for thirty. Why, then, have we not enough? Why do people die of starvation, or lead a miserable existence on the verge of it?

Why have millions upon millions to toil from morning to evening just to gain a mere crust of bread? Because of the absolute lack of Organisation by which
such labour should produce its effect, the absolute lack
of distribution, the absolute lack even of the very idea
that such things are possible. Nay, even to mention
such things, to say that they are possible, is criminal
with many. Madness could hardly go farther.

That selfishness has all to do with it I entirely deny.
The human race for ages upon ages has been enslaved
by ignorance and by interested persons whose object it
has been to confine the minds of men, thereby doing
more injury than if with infected hands they purposely
imposed disease on the heads of the people. Almost
worse than these, and at the present day as injurious,
are those persons incessantly declaring, teaching, and
impressing upon all that to work is man's highest condition. This falsehood is the interested superstition
of an age infatuated with money, which having accumulated it cannot even expend it in pageantry. It is a
falsehood propagated for the doubtful benefit of two
or three out of ten thousand. It is the lie of a morality founded on money only, and utterly outside and
having no association whatever with the human being
in itself. Many superstitions have been got rid of in
these days; time it is that this, the last and worst, were
eradicated.

At this hour, out of thirty-four millions who in-
habit this country, two-thirds—say twenty-two mil-

lions—live within thirty years of that abominable institution the poorhouse. That any human being should dare to apply to another the epithet "pauper" is, to me, the greatest, the vilest, the most unpardonable crime that could be committed. Each human being, by mere birth, has a birthright in this earth and all its productions; and if they do not receive it, then it is they who are injured, and it is not the "pauper"—oh, inexpressibly wicked word! —it is the well-to-do, who are the criminal classes. It matters not in the least if the poor be improvident, or drunken, or evil in any way. Food and drink, roof and clothes, are the inalienable right of every child born into the light. If the world does not provide it freely—not as a grudging gift but as a right, as a son of the house sits down to breakfast—then is the world mad. But the world is not mad, only in ignorance—an interested ignorance, kept up by strenuous exertions, from which infernal darkness it will, in course of time, emerge, marvelling at the past as a man wonders at and glories in the light who has escaped from blindness.

CHAINS

I hear Jefferies speaking directly to me. No membrane separates us.

I have questions. I see answers.

BW: What are we to do about the changing climate that now threatens life as we know it?

RJ: (I hear a strong, deep voice, nearly an echo.) *I am convinced that much more can be done, and that the length of time may be almost measurably shortened… There must be much more—there must be things which are at present unknown by whose aid advance may be made. Research proceeds upon the same old lines and runs in the ancient grooves.*

BW: I agree. Our "research" has many answers to our problem but none practical enough or political enough or cheap enough.

RJ: *Further research is restricted by the ultra-practical views which are alone deemed reasonable. Remember, experimentation is important but also limited, as it is built on what was previously found.*

BW: How do we move beyond this status quo, this assumption that we currently know all we need to know to solve all of our problems?

RJ: *There should be no limit placed on the mind. The purely ideal is as worthy of pursuit as the practical, and the mind is not to be pinned to dogmas of science any more than to dogmas of superstition.*

BW: What, if not science, if not by experimentation?

RJ: *Observation. If the eye is always watching, and the mind on the alert, ultimately chance supplies the solution.*

What Jefferies calls *chance* here might actually be inner consciousness—the psyche. He also calls it "super-sensuous reasoning," which he says, "arises from perceptions too delicate for analysis." Shamans—the men or women serving as the messengers between worlds, psychic healers in many traditional, ethnic religions throughout the world, refer to "Second Attention" through which information enters peripherally, inspired by the unconscious. Whereas "First Attention" is what we use to get through the day—find our keys, pay our bills, watch our weight, etc. The shamans believe that no significant change occurs in First Attention.

Jefferies is a huge proponent of idleness, because he believed that idleness was necessary for chance to work. From a young age, he refused to settle, or become a cog in the machine, part of the status quo. His neighbor, the village patriarch, called him "a lazy lout on the land."[6] Others thought him "incorrigibly lazy," and others, "half cracked."

Jefferies could be writing today when referring to the "old grooves" out of which our minds must be lifted if anything new is possible. We have access to new ideas once we divorce ourselves from the idea that

---

6. H.S. Salt quotes some of the neighbors who knew him during his youth.

limitless work is some form of glory, the main goal of our existence. It has become so clear to me that this modern—especially American—addiction to work and the material rewards we're promised in exchange must be disrupted, derailed, disconnected if we are to live truly meaningful lives, if a reasonable future is possible.

"So grown to its chains" is the world. Jefferies sees no hope for the masses and "to leave them is the only resource."

Sure, we have focused on ideas that make some lives easier and some very wealthy—automobiles, airplane travel, computers, bananas and strawberries in January come to mind—but few that make the world a better place, which is what Jefferies desired.

He desired the ideas that might free people from the slavery of an incessant need to work. Jefferies would be shocked to see that the world is becoming a massive marketplace run by a handful of multi-national corporations. Or not. Perhaps he saw it coming.

Jefferies holds two groups of people responsible: those who confine the minds of men, and those who promote the idea that work is man's highest condition. Those two groups, Jefferies claims, are "infatuated with money," having more than they can spend, even in "pageantry." Jefferies claims that those whose "morality is founded mainly on money" number two or three out of ten thousand. In his journal from January and February, 1887, he writes about the increase in millionaires, their lack of public spirit—"no trucks with food for the poor," "no science endowment," "no ships to the north," "simple downright selfishness"— "all the more needful to struggle against them, for unless we do we shall not even have the half loaf" (an idiom suggesting that getting part of what we want is better than nothing).

Were he alive today, Jefferies might have joined the Occupy movement, agreeing that those in the top "One Percent" of Americans are burying the rest of us under the weight of their wealth.

Jefferies ends the chapter confident that we'll one day emerge from this phase of "interested ignorance" in which we're seduced by a small percentage of the people who care more about money and power than anything else. We'll look back at this moment in time, amazed, looking "at the past as a man wonders at and glories in the light who has escaped from blindness."

I write Jefferies a letter:

Dear Mr. Jefferies,

I'm writing this to acknowledge the insight you had about where civilization was headed. Most of our "progress" is now killing the planet due to the combination of population (over 7 billion of us now compared to 1.5 billion during your life) and technology—chemically growing our food, burning all the fossil fuels powering our cars, heating our homes, and driving our industries. If you saw it, Mr. Jefferies, you wouldn't believe how so many people all over the world could be forced into such meaningless lives. (But we get better "bread and circuses"[7] in the form of professional sports, television game shows to participate in, fashions that will give them new meaning, religion promising them they'll get after death all they lacked during life, etc.)

The amounts of money being made are staggering, most of it by Wall Street financiers and crony-capitalist bankers, not by producing goods and services but by betting on what markets will or will not do and when. The farmers and educators—who do some of society's most valuable work—are near the bottom of the income pyramid. With extravagant money comes power and with power, more money: Corporate CEOs now make 450 times what they pay average workers; most members of the U.S. Congress are now millionaires; a presidential election campaign costs a billion dollars, most of which comes from corporations which the law treats as individuals. Most corporate CEOs focus only on the price of company stock, cutting them off from thinking about anything that might be logical, sustainable, or ethical.

Wandering—what you did most of your life—is still seen as a waste of time. In fact, where we live in Western America, most open or wild places where true wandering is still possible are being drilled and dug for the energy to fuel this massive carbon machine. The gases from burning this carbon are heating up the atmosphere and changing

---

7. "Give them bread and circuses and they will never revolt." Coined by the Roman poet Juvenal in the first century.

weather patterns, which could lead us into the next bottle-neck, dramatically reducing our numbers.

This madness was just beginning as you suffered and died. Efforts to protect the wild places that remain are always met with excuses: Economic—if we can't develop these natural resources many will lose their jobs; Security—if we can't get oil and gas out of our own land, we'll need to depend on those crazy towel-heads who only want us dead; or Cultural—God put these resources here for us and if we don't use them, they will go to waste. Wild lands are bad for business. Wildness is dangerous in the same way that some called yours a dangerous book, because people who understand wildness are less likely to conform to standards set for us by corporate America and more likely to use their super-sensuous reasoning (your term) for new ideas that might disrupt the status quo. Which is exactly what it needs.

You knew that this was coming. But you had no idea the extent to which our work ethic would drive us toward our own extinction. Can what you knew and wrote about inspire those of us living now to make the changes necessary? I doubt it. You knew you couldn't change those around you then, and the forces against these necessary changes have multiplied a hundred—a thousand—fold. "So grown to its chains," you said, 150 years ago. What about now? What do I do, Jefferies? I'll continue my own wandering. I'll move myself and those I love as far to the edge of all this as I can. And when I weaken and wonder and question my philosophy while pushing against the cul-

tural current trying to force me to conform I'll think of the story of your heart. And then I'll wander more.

I'll bet we would be friends were it not for the five generations separating us.

Sincerely,
Brooke

CHAPTER XI

~

This our earth produces not only a sufficiency, a superabundance, but in one year pours a cornucopia of good things forth, enough to fill us for many years in succession. The only reason we do not enjoy it is the want of rational organisation. I know, of course, and all who think know, that some labour or supervision will always be necessary, since the plough must travel the furrow and the seed must be sown; but I maintain that a tenth, nay, a hundredth, part of the labour and slavery now gone through will be sufficient, and that in the course of time, as organisation perfects itself and discoveries advance, even that part will diminish. For the rise and fall of the tides alone furnish forth sufficient power to do automatically all the labour that is done on the earth. Is ideal man, then, to be idle? I answer that, if so, I see no wrong, but a great good. I deny altogether that idleness is an evil, or that it produces evil, and I am well aware why the interested are so bitter against idleness—namely, because it gives time for thought, and if men had time to think their reign would come to an end. Idleness—that is, the absence of the necessity to work for subsistence—is a great good.

I hope succeeding generations will be able to be

ideal. I hope that nine-tenths of their time will be leisure time; that they may enjoy their days, and the earth, and the beauty of this beautiful world; that they may rest by the sea and dream; that they may dance and sing, and eat and drink. I will work towards that end with all my heart. If employment they must have—and the restlessness of the mind will insure that some will be followed—then they will find scope enough in the perfection of their physical frames, in the expansion of the mind, and in the enlargement of the soul. They shall not work for bread, but for their souls. I am willing to divide and share all I shall ever have for this purpose, though I think the end will rather be gained by organisation than by sharing alone.

In these material things, too, I think that we require another circle of ideas, and I believe that such ideas are possible, and, in a manner of speaking, exist. Let me exhort everyone to do their utmost to think outside and beyond our present circle of ideas. For every idea gained is a hundred years of slavery remitted. Even with the idea of organisation which promises most I am not satisfied, but endeavour to get beyond and outside it, so that the time now necessary may be shortened. Besides which, I see that many of our difficulties arise from obscure and remote causes—obscure like the shape of bones, for whose strange curves there is no familiar term. We must endeavour to understand the crookedness and unfamiliar curves of the conditions of life. Beyond that still there are other ideas.

Never, never rest contented with any circle of ideas, but always be certain that a wider one is still possible. For my thought is like a hyperbola that continually widens ascending.

For grief there is no known consolation. It is useless to fill our hearts with bubbles. A loved one gone is gone, and as to the future—even if there is a future—it is unknown. To assure ourselves otherwise is to soothe the mind with illusions; the bitterness of it is inconsolable. The sentiments of trust chipped out on tombstones are touching instances of the innate goodness of the human heart, which naturally longs for good, and sighs itself to sleep in the hope that, if parted, the parting is for the benefit of those that are gone. But these inscriptions are also awful instances of the deep intellectual darkness which presses still on the minds of men. The least thought erases them. There is no consolation. There is no relief. There is no hope certain; the whole system is a mere illusion. I, who hope so much, and am so rapt up in the soul, know full well that there is no certainty.

The tomb cries aloud to us—its dead silence presses on the drum of the ear like thunder, saying, Look at this, and erase your illusions; now know the extreme value of human life; reflect on this and strew human life with flowers; save every hour for the sunshine; let your labour be so ordered that in future times the loved ones may dwell longer with those who love them; open your minds; exalt your souls; widen the sympathies of your hearts; face the things that are now as you will face the reality of death; make joy real now to those you love, and help forward the joy of those yet to be born. Let these facts force the mind and the soul to the increase of thought, and the consequent remission of misery; so that those whose time it is to die may have enjoyed all that is possible in life. Lift up your mind and see now in this bitterness of parting, in this absence of certainty, the fact that there is no directing intelligence; remember that this death is not of old age, which no one living in the world has ever seen; remember that old age is possible, and perhaps even more than old age; and beyond these earthly things—what? None know. But let us, turning away from the illusion of a directing intelligence, look earnestly for something better than a god, seek for something higher than prayer, and lift our souls to be with the more than immortal now.

A river runs itself clear during the night, and in sleep thought becomes pellucid. All the hurrying to and fro, the unrest and stress, the agitation and confusion subside. Like a sweet pure spring, thought pours forth to meet the light, and is illumined to its depths. The dawn at my window ever causes a desire for larger thought, the recognition of the light at the moment of waking kindles afresh the wish for a broad day of the mind. There is a certainty that there are yet ideas further, and greater—that there is still a limitless beyond. I know at that moment that there is no limit to the things that may be yet in material and tangible shape besides the immaterial perceptions of the soul. The dim white light of the dawn speaks it. This prophet which has come with its wonders to the bedside of every human being for so many thousands of years faces me once again with the upheld finger of light. Where is the limit to that physical sign?

From space to the sky, from the sky to the hills, and the sea; to every blade of grass, to every leaf, to the smallest insect, to the million waves of ocean. Yet this earth itself appears but a mote in that sunbeam by which we are conscious of one narrow streak in the abyss. A beam crosses my silent chamber from the window, and atoms are visible in it; a beam slants between the fir-trees, and particles rise and fall within, and cross it while the air each side seems void. Through the heavens a beam slants, and we are aware of the star-stratum in which our earth moves. But what may be without that stratum? Certainly, it is not a void. This light tells us much, but I think in the course of time yet more delicate and subtle mediums than light may be found, and through these we shall see into the shadows of the sky. When will it be possible to be certain that the capacity of a single atom has been exhausted? At any moment, some fortunate incident may reveal a fresh power. One by one the powers of light have been unfolded.

After thousands of years the telescope opened the stars, the prism analysed the substance of the sun, the microscope showed the minute structure of the rocks and the tissues of living bodies. The winged men on the Assyrian bas-reliefs, the gods of the Nile, the chariot-borne immortals of Olympus, not the greatest of imagined beings ever possessed in fancied attributes one-tenth the power of light. As the swallows twitter, the dim white finger appears at my window full of wonders, such as all the wise men in twelve thousand precedent years never even hoped to conceive. But this is not all—light is not all; light conceals more than it reveals; light is the darkest shadow of the sky; besides light there are many other mediums yet to be explored. For thousands of years the sunbeams poured on the earth, full as now of messages, and light is not a hidden thing to be searched out with difficulty. Full in the faces of men the rays came with their intelligence from the sun when the papyri were painted beside the ancient Nile, but they were not understood.

This hour, rays or undulations of more subtle mediums are doubtless pouring on us over the wide earth, unrecognised, and full of messages and intelligence from the unseen. Of these we are this day as ignorant as those who painted the papyri were of light. There is an infinity of knowledge yet to be known, and beyond that an infinity of thought. No mental instrument even has yet been invented by which researches can be carried direct to the object. Whatever has been found has been discovered by fortunate accident; in looking for one thing another has been chanced on. A reasoning process has yet to be invented by which to go straight to the desired end. For now the slightest particle is enough to throw the search aside, and the most minute circumstance sufficient to conceal obvious and brilliantly shining truths. One summer evening, sitting by my window, I watched for the first star to appear, knowing the position of the brightest in the southern sky. The dusk came on, grew deeper, but the star did not shine. By-and-by, other stars less bright appeared, so that it could not be the sunset which obscured the expected one. Finally, I considered that I must have mistaken its position, when suddenly a puff of air blew through the branch of a pear tree, which overhung the window, a leaf moved, and there was the star behind the leaf.

At present, the endeavour to make discoveries is like gazing at the sky up through the boughs of an oak. Here a beautiful star shines clearly; here a constellation is hidden by a branch; a universe by a leaf. Some mental instrument or organon is required to enable us to distinguish between the leaf which may be removed and a real void; when to cease to look in one direction, and to work in another. Many men of broad brow and great intellect lived in the days of ancient Greece, but for lack of the accident of a lens, and of knowing the way to use a prism, they could but conjecture imperfectly. I am in exactly the position they were when I look beyond light. Outside my present knowledge I am exactly in their condition. I feel that there are infinities to be known, but they are hidden by a leaf. If anyone says to himself that the telescope, and the microscope, the prism, and other discoveries have made all plain, then he is in the attitude of those ancient priests who worshipped the scarabaeus or beetle. So, too, it is with thought; outside our present circle of ideas I believe there is an infinity of idea. All this that has been effected with light has been done by bits of glass—mere bits of shaped glass, quickly broken, and made of flint, so that by the rude flint our subtlest ideas are gained. Could we employ the ocean as a lens, and force truth from the sky, even then I think there would be much more beyond.

Natural things are known to us only under two conditions—matter and force, or matter and motion. A third, a fourth, a fifth—no one can say how many conditions—may exist in the ultra-stellar space, and such other conditions may equally exist about us now unsuspected. Something which is neither matter nor force is difficult to conceive, yet, I think, it is certain that there are other conditions. When the mind succeeds in entering on a wider series, or circle of ideas, other conditions would appear natural enough. In this effort upwards I claim the assistance of the soul—the mind of the mind. The eye sees, the mind deliberates on what it sees, the soul understands the operation of the mind. Before a bridge is built, or a structure erected, or an interoceanic canal made, there must be a plan, and before a plan the thought in the mind. So that it is correct to say the mind bores tunnels through the mountains, bridges the rivers, and constructs the engines which are the pride of the world.

This is a wonderful tool, but it is capable of work yet more wonderful in the exploration of the heavens. Now the soul is the mind of the mind. It can build and construct and look beyond and penetrate space, and create. It is the keenest, the sharpest tool possessed by man. But what would be said if a carpenter about to commence a piece of work examined his tools and deliberately cast away that with the finest edge? Such is the conduct of those who reject the inner mind or psyche altogether. So great is the value of the soul that it seems to me, if the soul lived and received its aspirations it would not matter if the material universe melted away as snow. Many turn aside the instant the soul is mentioned, and I sympathise with them in one sense; they fear lest, if they acknowledge it, they will be fettered by mediaeval conditions. My contention is that the restrictions of the mediaeval era should entirely be cast into oblivion, but the soul recognised and employed. Instead of slurring over the soul, I desire to see it at its highest perfection.

STARS

The sun rises between the dark peaks in the southeast end of the Castle Valley and light instantly floods the main room of our house. The exact moment that light penetrates the glass enveloping the house, it turns to heat. Miracle!

Many of those critical of *The Story of My Heart* and Jefferies in general say his writing is repetitious. I have to agree. This chapter has more about "soul" and the expanding "circles of ideas," the eternal Now, all of which I hurry past. I've come to trust that between the recurring ideas Jefferies threads throughout this book, there is always something new. This is the fourth time I've read this chapter, and I realize I've missed seeing his ideas about light and possible energy sources until now. I am beginning to understand the connection between the fourth idea, more soul, something beyond deity, and higher than prayer, that Jefferies longed for, and the climate crises our species currently faces.

Jefferies calls that first morning light a prophet because it carries the "desire for larger thought" and its capacity to "kindle afresh the wish for a broad day of the mind." He watches one sunbeam enter his room and notices what he calls atoms floating in it… and then wonders about the capacity of a single atom, which he predicts that by "some fortunate accident may reveal a fresh power."

Nuclear power—how could he have known?

Later, he contemplates the sunrays constantly "pouring on us over the wide earth, unrecognized, and full of messages and intelligence from the unseen."

Solar power? I doubt it, but that's what I think reading this chapter.

Jefferies was critical of his time, the late nineteenth century, known for innovation and technology and economic growth. Coal-generated electrical and steam power and land-clearing for development launched unprecedented quantities of carbon into the atmosphere. Analysis of ice cores show that the earth's atmosphere contained approximately 280 parts per million of greenhouse gases until the late 1800s when that number began to dramatically increase toward 390 ppm, where it is today. Scientists suggest anything more than 350 ppm will result in an unrecognizable, unpredictable, and certainly uncomfortable future.

Philip Drew, in his 1967 paper "Richard Jefferies and the English Countryside," suggests that Jefferies was a social critic, due to his extraordinarily relevant observations on the Industrial Revolution. Drew credits Jefferies with being one who, amid the "universal rejoicing and the advance of humanity" asked his culture to "stand fast for a moment and consider what direction the march of Progress is taking." What are we really gaining? What are we in danger of losing?

The Story of My Heart is a political book about economics and according to Drew, "how men ought to live, what alternatives can be found or imagined to the desperate Victorian struggle for advancement."

In *The Story of My Heart,* and in many of his other writing, Jefferies compares the infinite abundance of nature[8] with civilization—what he calls "House Life"—and its "thrift and economy and accumulation," which he sees as not only contrary to nature, but also destructive to nature. For Jefferies, nature means abundance and civilization requires thrift.

We're still asking those same questions: Are our technological advancements real gains? What are we giving up for them? Now, generations further down the same path, we may be forgetting what we're losing.

The "two or three in ten thousand" has grown to the One Percent, or one hundred in ten thousand, the Occupy movement symbolically rose up against. This increase seems directly related to the rise in the amount of greenhouse gas in the atmosphere from then (280 ppm) to now (400 ppm). Unless we do something to "struggle against" the rich—revolt?—or find other ways to lower greenhouse gases, we're fucked.

Jefferies tells of an evening looking at the sky waiting for what he knew would be the first star to appear. "The dusk came on," he writes,

---

8. "There is no enough in nature. It is one vast prodigality. It is a feast. There is no economy: it is all one immense extravagance. It is all giving, giving, giving: no saving, no penury; a golden shower of good things is for ever descending. I love beyond all things to contemplate this indescribable lavishness" (Jefferies).

But the star did not shine…Finally, I considered that I must have mistaken its position, when suddenly a puff of air blew through the branch of a pear-tree which overhung the window, a leaf moved, and there was the star behind the leaf…Some mental instrument… is required to enable us to distinguish between the leaf…and a real void.

I wish it were this simple. Perhaps in Jefferies' day the answers were hidden temporarily until exposed by changing conditions. What we need now might be found only if we're willing to travel deep into the void, which may be more internal than not.

No moon yet tonight in Castle Valley, where our laws insure that any outdoor lights will point down to protect the darkness. The stars begin to appear, not gradually with the dying light, but born, the first and brightest giving birth to the young who will soon fill the sky with a thousand generations.

CHAPTER XII

◦

S ubtle as the mind is, it can affect little without knowledge. It cannot construct a bridge, or a building, or make a canal, or work a problem in algebra, unless it is provided with information. This is obvious, and yet some say, What can you effect by the soul? I reply because it has had no employment. Mediaeval conditions kept it in slumber: science refuses to accept it. We are taught to employ our minds, and furnished with materials. The mind has its logic and exercise of geometry, and thus assisted brings a great force to the solution of problems. The soul remains untaught, and can effect little.

I consider that the highest purpose of study is the education of the soul or psyche. It is said that there is no proof of the existence of the soul, but, arguing on the same grounds, there is no proof of the existence of the mind, which is not a tangible thing. For myself, I feel convinced that there is a soul, a mind of the mind—and that it really exists. Now, glancing at the state of wild and uneducated men, it is evident that they work with their hands and make various things almost instinctively. But when they arrive at the idea of mind, and say to themselves, I possess a mind, then they think and proceed farther, forming designs and constructions both tangible and mental.

Next then, when we say, I have a soul, we can proceed to shape things yet further, and to see deeper, and
penetrate the mystery. By denying the existence and the
power of the soul—refusing to employ it—we should
go back more than twelve thousand written years of human history. But instead of this, I contend, we should
endeavour to go forward, and to discover a fourth Idea,
and after that a fifth, and onwards continually.

I will not permit myself to be taken captive by
observing physical phenomena, as many evidently are.
Some gases are mingled and produce a liquid; certainly it is worth careful investigation, but it is no more
than the revolution of a wheel, which is so often seen
that it excites no surprise, though, in truth, as wonderful. So is all motion, and so is a grain of sand; there
is nothing that is not wonderful; as, for instance, the
fact of the existence of things at all. But the intense
concentration of the mind on mechanical effects appears often to render it incapable of perceiving anything that is not mechanical. Some compounds are
observed to precipitate crystals, all of which contain
known angles. Thence it is argued that all is mechanical, and that action occurs in set ways only. There is a
tendency to lay it down as an infallible law that because we see these things therefore everything else
that exists in space must be or move exactly in the
same manner. But I do not think that because crystals
are precipitated with fixed angles therefore the whole

universe is necessarily mechanical. I think there are things exempt from mechanical rules. The restriction of thought to purely mechanical grooves blocks progress in the same way as the restrictions of mediaeval superstition. Let the mind think, dream, imagine: let it have perfect freedom. To shut out the soul is to put us back more than twelve thousand years.

Just as outside light, and the knowledge gained from light, there are, I think, other mediums from which, in times to come, intelligence will be obtained, so outside the mental and the spiritual ideas we now possess I believe there exists a whole circle of ideas. In the conception of the idea that there are others, I lay claim to another idea.

The mind is infinite and able to understand everything that is brought before it; there is no limit to its understanding. The limit is in the littleness of the things and the narrowness of the ideas which have been put for it to consider. For the philosophies of old time past and the discoveries of modern research are as nothing to it. They do not fill it. When they have been read, the mind passes on, and asks for more. The utmost of them, the whole together, make a mere nothing. These things have been gathered together by immense labour, labour so great that it is a weariness to think of it; but yet, when all is summed up and written, the mind receives it all as easily as the hand picks flowers. It is like one sentence—read and gone.

The mind requires more, and more, and more. It is

so strong that all that can be put before it is devoured in a moment. Left to itself it will not be satisfied with an invisible idol any more than with a wooden one. An idol whose attributes are omnipresence, omnipotence, and so on, is no greater than light or electricity, which are present everywhere and all-powerful, and from which perhaps the thought arose. Prayer which receives no reply must be pronounced in vain. The mind goes on and requires more than these, something higher than prayer, something higher than a god.

I have been obliged to write these things by an irresistible impulse, which has worked in me since early youth. They have not been written for the sake of argument, still less for any thought of profit, rather indeed the reverse. They have been forced from me by earnestness of heart, and they express my most serious convictions. For seventeen years they have been lying in my mind, continually thought of and pondered over. I was not more than eighteen when an inner and esoteric meaning began to come to me from all the visible universe, and indefinable aspirations filled me. I found them in the grass fields, under the trees, on the hilltops, at sunrise, and in the night. There was a deeper meaning everywhere. The sun burned with it, the broad front of morning beamed with it; a deep feeling entered me while gazing at the sky in the azure noon, and in the star-lit evening.

I was sensitive to all things, to the earth under, and the star-hollow round about; to the least blade of grass, to the largest oak. They seemed like exterior nerves and veins for the conveyance of feeling to me. Sometimes a very ecstasy of exquisite enjoyment of the entire visible universe filled me. I was aware that in reality the feeling and the thought were in me, and not in the earth or sun; yet I was more conscious of it when in company with these. A visit to the sea increased the strength of the original impulse. I began to make efforts to express these thoughts in writing, but could not succeed to my own liking. Time went on, and harder experiences, and the pressure of labour came, but in no degree abated the fire of first thought. Again and again I made resolutions that I would write it, in some way or other, and as often failed. I could express any other idea with ease, but not this. Once especially I remember, in a short interval of distasteful labour, walking away to a spot by a brook which skirts an ancient Roman wall, and there trying to determine and really commence to work. Again I failed. More time, more changes, and still the same thought running beneath everything. At last, in 1880, in the old castle of Pevensey, under happy circumstances, once more I resolved, and actually did write down a few notes. Even then I could not go on, but I kept the notes (I had destroyed all former beginnings), and in the end, two years afterwards, commenced this book.

After all this time and thought it is only a fragment, and a fragment scarcely hewn. Had I not made it personal I could scarcely have put it into any shape at all. But I felt that I could no longer delay, and that it must be done, however imperfectly. I am only too conscious of its imperfections, for I have as it were seventeen years of consciousness of my own inability to express this, the idea of my life. I can only say that many of these short sentences are the result of long-continued thought. One of the greatest difficulties I have encountered is the lack of words to express ideas. By the word soul, or psyche, I mean that inner consciousness which aspires. By prayer, I do not mean a request for anything preferred to a deity; I mean intense soul-emotion, intense aspiration. The word immortal is very inconvenient, and yet there is no other to convey the idea of soul-life. Even these definitions are deficient, and I must leave my book as a whole to give its own meaning to its words.

Time has gone on, and still, after so much pondering, I feel that I know nothing, that I have not yet begun; I have only just commenced to realise the immensity of thought, which lies outside the knowledge of the senses. Still, on the hills and by the seashore, I seek and pray deeper than ever. The sun burns southwards over the sea and before the wave runs its shadow, constantly slipping on the advancing slope till it curls and covers its dark image at the shore. Over the rim of the horizon waves are flowing as high and wide as those that break upon the beach. These that come to me and beat the trembling shore are like the thoughts that have been known so long; like the ancient, iterated, and reiterated thoughts that have broken on the strand of mind for thousands of years. Beyond and over the horizon I feel that there are other waves of ideas unknown to me, flowing as the stream of ocean flows. Knowledge of facts is limitless: they lie at my feet innumerable like the countless pebbles; knowledge of thought so circumscribed! Ever the same thoughts come that have been written down centuries and centuries.

Let me launch forth and sail over the rim of the sea yonder, and when another rim arises over that, and again and onwards into an ever-widening ocean of idea and life. For with all the strength of the wave, and its succeeding wave, the depth and race of the tide, the clear definition of the sky; with all the subtle power of the great sea, there rises an equal desire. Give me life strong and full as the brimming ocean; give me thoughts wide as its plain; give me a soul beyond these. Sweet is the bitter sea by the shore where the faint blue pebbles are lapped by the green-grey wave, where the wind-quivering foam is loath to leave the lashed stone. Sweet is the bitter sea, and the clear green in which the gaze seeks the soul, looking through the glass into itself. The sea thinks for me as I listen and ponder; the sea thinks, and every boom of the wave repeats my prayer.

Sometimes I stay on the wet sands as the tide rises, listening to the rush of the lines of foam in layer upon layer; the wash swells and circles about my feet, I have my hands in it, I lift a little in my hollowed palm, I take the life of the sea to me. My soul rising to the immensity utters its desire-prayer with all the strength of the sea. Or, again, the full stream of ocean beats upon the shore, and the rich wind feeds the heart, the sun burns brightly; the sense of soul-life burns in me like a torch.

Leaving the shore I walk among the trees; a cloud passes, and the sweet short rain comes mingled with sunbeams and flower-scented air. The finches sing among the fresh green leaves of the beeches. Beautiful it is, in summer days, to see the wheat wave, and the long grass foam, flecked of flower yield and return to the wind. My soul of itself always desires; these are to it as fresh food. I have found in the hills another valley grooved in prehistoric times, where, climbing to the top of the hollow, I can see the sea. Down in the hollow I look up; the sky stretches over, the sun burns as it seems but just above the hill, and the wind sweeps onward. As the sky extends beyond the valley, so I know that there are ideas beyond the valley of my thought; I know that there is something infinitely higher than deity. The great sun burning in the sky, the sea, the firm earth, all the stars of night are feeble—all, all the cosmos is feeble; it is not strong enough to utter my prayer-desire. My soul cannot reach to its full desire of prayer. I need no earth, or sea, or sun to think my thought. If my thought-part—the psyche—were entirely separated from the body, and from the earth,

I should of myself desire the same. In itself my soul desires; my existence, my soul-existence is in itself my prayer, and so long as it exists so long will it pray that I may have the fullest soul-life.

LEAP

What happened during the night? I woke up agitated, frustrated, a bit pissed off. I settle with my coffee on a bench outside in the dramatic morning sun. The frustration I feel must be but a fraction of what Jefferies was feeling as he neared the end of this book, his life. I'm ready to start making notes on the last chapter, still uncertain about the force behind my obsession, with him, this book, the story of Jefferies' heart. Immersed in thick dense desert quiet that throbs and hums, where everything moves slowly, I wonder if I'm using Jefferies simply to support and justify my own philosophy, to solidify my beliefs and my rationalizations. I hope I'm not in the same place I was in when I began.

Jefferies believed that progress is impossible if our thoughts are restricted to "purely mechanical grooves," suggesting man-made pathways we're intended to travel along without questioning, which are difficult to escape—train tracks, perhaps. At birth, we get a train ticket. The direction, route, and destination of our lives are all predetermined.

One moment I am sitting still on the bench, the warm sun penetrating my forehead, and the next I am inside a train car. Of all the trains, this is the best train. Here I am with all the smart, progressive people, moving forward toward the future. But I know that where this train is going is wrong. I'm wearing headphones listening to music, when suddenly I hear Richard Jefferies' voice. "Get off the train," he says. I look around. "Get off that train, now," the voice says. Then it gets weird. I know where the train is going and that I should get off, but I'm afraid. I know there's a future where all life thrives, but I've not heard of a train that goes there. Then I rationalize. Perhaps where we're headed won't be as bad as I fear; after all, lots of thought is going into getting this train safely to the future. Everyone on this train recycles and drives a Prius. We're all members of The Nature Conservancy. We're all doing our own small part. The train has been retrofitted for the future—it runs on solar power, serves organic food in the galley, and has waterless urinals. Many good, incremental changes have been made, but the train is still headed in the wrong direction.

"When are you going to get off of the train?"

I look out the window and see that we're passing through green hills and a valley filled with trees, a stream running between them. The train isn't going fast, and if I jump, I might get scraped up or sprain my ankle. I probably won't die. But I've spent my life, 62 years, on this train. Everything I've read and written and thought about—everything I've experienced—is on this train and too bulky to take with me.

Leaving it all behind, I get up from my seat and hurry through the car. I am light and quick and a thousand thoughts move through my head. This train will stay on this track until it crashes into an insurmountable obstacle—a landslide or a different train moving in the opposite direction. Finally, I come to the door at the end of the car. I push it open and look out. I see the hills and the valley between them. Below me, I see tall grass growing in what I hope is soft earth. I hear Jefferies: "If the eye is always watching, and the mind on the alert, ultimately chance supplies the solution."

A meadowlark calling from a fence post returns me to my body, the house, and the bench, and I move back inside.

I open *The Story of My Heart* to Chapter XII and immediately the six times I've circled the word "soul" jump off of the first page. I don't ever need to see that word (or "soul-life") again. And, I need a day off.

Then the thought strikes me: this book is unlike any I've ever read. I trust what Jefferies wrote in this book. I've spent years reading it off and on, and two years trying to make sense of it. I'm still not sure why.

Soul. Jefferies uses the word again and again, interchangeably with "psyche" and "inner consciousness." I was taught during my early days in church that "soul" referred to a committed Mormon, as in "Brigham Young entered the Salt Lake Valley along with 148 other souls," but also, "soul" is where one's spirit and body unite. I've experienced "soul"—moments of intense clarity I feel deep in my bones; emotional electricity flashing along my spine.

Soul, I'm suddenly aware, is my connection to the

earth, but more. Soul is the *conduit* between the earth and me, through which energy and nourishment flow. This is what Jefferies has been trying to tell me. There's more. Insight flows from the earth to me, up through my soul. This is the source of my obsession. Perhaps pure obsession is the earth telling us how it will make the best use of us.

A question rises up in my throat, pressurized like bile: "So what are you going to do with what you know?"

I take a deep breath. I am leaving my past behind and moving into a new phase of life. As if I've just torn off clothes that were too tight, I feel loose and free. I read Chapter XII fresh. Each time I read the word "soul" I think of my own and read it as if Jefferies were writing directly to me. "What can you effect by the soul?" becomes "what can you effect by YOUR soul."

"The highest purpose of study is the education of YOUR soul," Jefferies says to me.

My soul, according to Jefferies, is "the mind of [my] mind."

It can build and construct and look beyond and penetrate space, and create. It is the keenest, the sharpest tool possessed by man. But what would be said if a carpenter about to commence a piece of work examined his tools and deliberately cast away that with the finest edge?

I'm not a carpenter. I'm a conservationist who is

discovering my soul's vast potential. Now, I must master this "tool with the finest edge," and use it to make something meaningful and beautiful, something that lasts. I will find the words to say that this is beyond magic. I will look for evidence that this is true, and explanations for skeptics. I will find the language that empowers those who've been told they have no power. This is what Jefferies intended when his life was cut short.

Looking out from the train, I see Terry in the distance waiting for me. Tall grasses bend toward her in the stiff breeze. I am afraid, but as if I no longer have a choice, I jump.

NATURAL PRAYERS

Scott Slovic

NATURAL PRAYERS

Not being of theological bent, I tend to draw a blank or pull back when talk turns to formal religion. The thought of going inside a building and reading a holy, old text or listening to an authority tell me how to worship an abstract deity doesn't turn me on, doesn't feel quite right. For me, as John Muir famously put it, "going out is really going in," a line I have long interpreted as saying that we delve into our deepest spiritual and psychological reality by going out into the world of nature.

John Muir, Henry Beston, Aldo Leopold, Wendell Berry, Gary Snyder, Barry Lopez, Richard Nelson, Sigurd Olson, Scott Russell Sanders, Chet Raymo, and, yes, Terry Tempest Williams and Brooke Williams—these are some of the names that come to mind when I think of how the process of going out into the world guides the human consciousness toward a richer, more meaningful contemplation of what it means to be alive and human. And Rick Bass, Janisse Ray, Bill McKibben, Kathleen Dean Moore, Robert Michael Pyle, George Venn, Brenda Peterson, and Linda Hogan. And Tim Winton, Jean Giono, Tao Yuanming, Liu Kexiang, Zakes Mda, and Miyazawa Kenji. This list goes on and on, and the more I think about these writers and their words, the more I realize that they are, in much of their work, revealing the "stories of their hearts," their truest emotional responses to the essential qualities of their lives in relation to the not-human not-self. Yes, these writers are "authorities," but authorities whose words propel readers beyond their texts, not merely into isolated human discourse and traditions.

It's likely that few of these writers have read Richard Jefferies, not having lucked into a copy of his hard-to-find book, as Terry and Brooke did. But they are Jefferies' kindred spirits. As are the British Romantic poets, Charles Darwin, and even eighteenth-century writers such as Jonathan Edwards, whose "Personal Narrative," in which he offers the double entendre "prayer seemed to be natural to me," abounds with stories of solitary, joyous engagement with woods and waters and fields.

Religion of course, according to such scholars as Joseph Campbell, comes from *re-ligare,* to re-connect. I interpret religion as the quest for fundamental re-connection with something that ultimately matters. I care less about connecting with the merely human than about touching base with something that clarifies my small self by placing it, placing me, in fuller context. For me, religion means nature ... and the human words that reveal the nature of that which exceeds me.

No Nature declares Gary Snyder in the title of his 1992 poetry collection, but he does not mean literally that there is no such thing as a natural world. Rather, he gestures koan-like toward the idea that there is no separate nature from human culture. "Both together, one big empty house," he persists—in the truest ecological sense, the human household exists in sync with the larger household of the planet and the universe. There are no real or visible boundaries. This is what Robinson Jeffers was getting at when he wrote "not man apart." Lately, among scholars in the field of ecocriticism, and more broadly in the environmental humanities, people are talking about "the New Materialism," using terms like "agentic capacity" and "intra-action" and "transcorporeality" to describe this feeling of being connected to the vibrant forces of the universe. We yearn to be engaged with otherness almost to the point where difference disappears. The 1970s philosophical movement known as Deep Ecology pushed toward such erasure, calling for "all beings" to be of equal stature. More recently, this same impulse has led to "object-oriented ontology"—what Timothy Morton poses as "really deep ecology"—a vision of reality as an intricate mesh of entities.

Not being the type to attend church or synagogue or mosque, I've never leaned toward prayer in the traditional sense. Rather than petitioning some abstract force for support and encouragement, my motto has always been "just do it." Perhaps this corporate phrase is simply in the air and water in my home state of Oregon.

But I've come to realize that the concept of prayer has the capacity to mean more than supplication. When I look for definitions or explanations of prayer, I find references to intentional communication with "a deity," with "an object of worship," and with "a spiritual entity." But I also find hints that certain kinds of "action," including yoga, might be prayerful insofar as they embody our practices of devotion to the earth.

The reason I find myself thinking about prayer, having never consciously uttered a prayer in my life, is that I recently reread Richard Jefferies' *The Story of My Heart*, which I last contemplated and annotated in preparation for my Ph.D. comprehensive exam in March 1988. Tucked in between Gerard Manley Hopkins' "God's Grandeur" (and other poems) and Robert Louis Stevenson's *Treasure Island* on my eleven-page reading list is Jefferies' memoir of solitary rambles among the hilly fields of West Brighton, England, which I imagine to be somewhat like the green, rolling farmlands of the Palouse, where I now live, on the border of Washington and Idaho in the inland Northwest of the United States. No sooner did I re-open Jefferies' book after a hiatus of twenty-six years than I came across these lines:

> I was utterly alone with the sun and the earth. Lying down on the grass, I spoke in my my soul to the earth, the sun, the air, and the distant sea far beyond sight…. By all these I prayed; I felt an emotion of the soul beyond all definition; prayer is a puny thing to it, and the word is a rude sign to the feeling, but I know no other (chapter 1, paragraph 4).

This idea of making tangible contact with the physical world brings to mind John Muir atop a thrashing Douglas Spruce during a Sierra windstorm (*The Mountains of California*), Scott Russell Sanders hugging a maple in his Bloomington backyard (*Staying Put*), Terry Tempest Williams immersing herself in the rushing snowmelt of the Colorado Plateau (*Desert Quartet*)—and from the physical act comes an emotional reaction. Where would we be without emotions? I often feel that one of the principle functions of the literary genre I call "environmental literature" is to return us, as writers and readers, to an appreciation of the emotive dimension of our minds. In his preface to the book *Numbers and Nerves: Information and Meaning in a World of Data*, which I recently completed with my father, the psychologist Paul Slovic, Robert Michael Pyle writes: "We know from the start that we are creatives of compassion and feeling, but also animals of analysis and measurement." As we make our way into the twenty-first century, some 130 years following the original publication of *The Story of My Heart*, Pyle reminds us that in order to "set the world aright ... we need all the math we can marshall for our case, which is the case of the earth and its living things, including ourselves. And we also need all the song, dance, poetry, and emotion we can muster...."

My scholarly notes on Jefferies from a quarter-century ago refer to such categories as personal nature essay, natural theology, hermeneutic sermon, walking narrative, exploration narrative, and the calendar. But after a career spent contemplating, cultivating, and celebrating environmental thought and expression throughout the world, I am now captivated by Richard Jefferies' plainspoken stories of simple contact with the earth, his effort to capture private emotional responses to such contact, and his struggle to find words to match the intensity of his experience. I would now classify this book as a volume of "natural prayers."

The Story of My Heart is so rich that I can hardly bear to read more than a few lines in one sitting. In fact, I feel slightly embarrassed to peruse Jefferies' candid lines, as if I am eavesdropping on the author's private whisperings. When I encounter these stories, I find myself not drawn into language, but driven out in the world, newly attentive, my own inner monologue stilled and then restarted.

I read Jefferies. I write these words. I walk outside to the grass, where I sit with my dog, listening to bees, watching tulips nod in the slight breeze, occasionally hearing traffic in the distance.

— Scott Slovic

ACKNOWLEDGMENTS

Our deepest gratitude is reserved for Jackie Burnett, owner of the magical bookstore Prints and Reprints, located on 31 Main Street in Stonington, Maine. It was here we found that small precious copy of *The Story of My Heart* that changed the quality of our own hearts as we absorbed Richard Jefferies' words and ideas into our bloodstream.

Kirsten Johanna Allen and Mark Bailey, publishers of Torrey House Press, listened to our enthusiasm about Jefferies and had the vision of bringing his words back into print for a contemporary readership to enjoy. We also appreciate the editorial care of Anne Terashima. The fact that Mark Bailey is the grandson of Camille Cazier Bailey, aunt to Kathryn Blackett Tempest, to whom this book is dedicated, makes it all the sweeter knowing our collaboration exists in the realm of family.

Scott Slovic, a pioneering scholar of nature writing and founder of the Association for the Study of Literature and Environment (ASLE), generously agreed to write the afterword, placing Richard Jefferies not only in a literary context but offering insight into his work as part of the lineage of Emerson and Thoreau and Edward Abbey. Scott's friendship is long and deep and cherished.

We are also indebted to the support of Gary Lawless and Beth Leonard, owners of Gulf of Maine

Books; Mariah Hughs and Nick Sichterman of Blue Hill Books; and Jan Sloan of The King's English Bookshop in Salt Lake City for her careful reading of the galleys. This book is another grace note alive in the world because of the leadership of independent publishers and booksellers.

Jean Saunders, Honorary Secretary of the Richard Jefferies Society, brought the author to life as she gave us a personal tour of the Richard Jefferies Museum in Coate Swindon, England. Not only did she provide tea and biscuits during our stay on the cold, overcast days in February, but she shared story after story of Jefferies' life and longings passed down through the ages. Her intimate knowledge of his work and her commitment to his legacy as a writer, activist, and philosopher inspired us. Saunders' work as an environmental activist to maintain the integrity of Jefferies' landscape now threatened by urban development is a hands-on example of how issues of a just economy and ecology, so important to Jefferies' work, is especially relevant today as conservationists and devotees of Richard Jefferies strive to protect the wildlands and wildlife surrounding Coate's Farm and their community. Their story becomes all of ours.

We also wish to acknowledge the dedication of the Board of Trustees of the Richard Jefferies Society and the helpful staff at the Pear Tree Inn in Purton, England, who took care of us during our extended stay.

Our patient friends deserve praise: Lyn Dalebout,

Alexandra Fuller, Jack Turner, Lee and Ed Riddell, Eleanor and Bill Hedden among them, alongside our sister Becky Williams Thomas, endured our obsession with Jefferies over many a late night dinner.

And lastly, to Richard Jefferies, our deepest affection and respect for his prescient knowledge of people in place and all that contributes "to the fullest soul-life."

ABOUT THE AUTHORS

RICHARD JEFFERIES was born November 6, 1848, on Coate Farm, near Swindon, England. The son of a poor farmer, his life-long encounters with the countryside near his childhood home formed the basis for his five hundred essays, and thirty books of fiction, natural history, and memoir. In his "spiritual autobiography," *The Story of My Heart* (1883), he explores both his outer and inner landscapes. This book is prophetic in its critique of our mechanized world and how it leads to social injustices and ecological destruction. It gained Jefferies the reputation of a nature mystic and philosopher concerned with "soul-life." He died August 14, 1887, after years of suffering with tuberculosis in Goring-on-the-Sea, near Worthington, England. He was thirty-eight years old.

BROOKE WILLIAMS is the author of four books including *Halflives: Reconciling Work and Wildness*. His work has been published in *Outside*, *The Huffington Post*, *Orion*, and *Saltfront*. He has spent the last thirty years advocating for wilderness, most recently with the Southern Utah Wilderness Alliance in Moab, Utah. He and Terry Tempest Williams have been married for forty years and divide their time between Utah and Wyoming.

TERRY TEMPEST WILLIAMS is author of fourteen books including the environmental literature classic, *Refuge: An Unnatural History of Family and Place.* Her most recent book is *When Women Were Birds.* She is the Annie Clark Tanner Scholar at the University of Utah's Environmental Humanities Graduate Program and also teaches at Dartmouth College. Her work has been translated and anthologized around the world.

SCOTT SLOVIC is professor of literature and environment and chair of the Department of English at the University of Idaho. As founding president of the Association of the Study of Literature and the Environment, he has written hundreds of articles and co-authored, edited, and written twenty-one books in the field of ecocriticism including *Seeking Awareness in American Nature Writing.* He lives in Moscow, Idaho.

TORREY HOUSE PRESS

*The economy is a wholly owned subsidiary
of the environment, not the other way around.*
—Senator Gaylord Nelson, founder of Earth Day

Love of the land inspires Torrey House Press and the books we publish. From literature and the environment and Western Lit to topical nonfiction about land related issues and ideas, we strive to increase appreciation for the importance of natural landscape through the power of pen and story. Through our *2% to the West* program, Torrey House Press donates two percent of sales to not-for-profit environmental organizations and funds a scholarship for up-and-coming writers at colleges throughout the West.

WWW.TORREYHOUSE.COM